# The Gospel in the Willows

*Forty Meditations*

Inspired by
*The Wind in the Willows*

## LESLIE J. FRANCIS

DARTON·LONGMAN+TODD

First published in 2009 by
Darton, Longman and Todd Ltd
1 Spencer Court
140 – 142 Wandsworth High Street
London SW18 4JJ

ISBN 978-0-232-52772-8

A catalogue record for this book is available from the British Library.

Produced by Judy Linard
Set in 10.5 on 13 pt Goudy Old Style
Printed and bound in Great Britain by
Athenaeum Press, Gateshead, Tyne & Wear

# Contents

# Preface

In *The Wind in the Willows* Kenneth Grahame crafted a text that has stood the test of time. It is a text that captivates the young and continues to enchant adults. Ratty, Mole and Toad have established their place deep in the hearts, minds and souls of successive generations. Grahame's insights both into the altruism and generosity and into the selfishness and stupidity of the human race ring true time and time again. Grahame's skilful use of language and wise choice of images rewards reflection and re-reading. There is without doubt a gospel message in the Willows.

As a young preacher I would often turn to *The Wind in the Willows* for inspiration and for illustration. I would select passages from Kenneth Grahame's writings to interpret and to communicate the gospel text. According to this method the gospel text was primary and the narrative by Kenneth Grahame always secondary. My understanding of the hermeneutical process has matured since then.

What I have set out to do in *The Gospel in the Willows* is to establish a more balanced conversation between Kenneth Grahame's text and the gospel narratives traditionally associated with Matthew, Mark, Luke and John. In this conversation I have allowed Kenneth

Grahame to speak first and then identified an appropriate passage from the Gospels to function as the conversation partner. In the ensuing conversation, I have invited both sources of narrative to illuminate each other. Throughout, my aim has been to enrich appreciation of what it means to be human (created in the image of God) and to live life aware of the dawning reign of God (initiated in the saving work of Christ).

The potential for such conversation between Kenneth Grahame's text and the Gospel narratives is enormous. In order to illustrate the method at work, I have structured five conversations for each of the first eight chapters of *The Wind in the Willows*. This structure generates forty conversations all told. While these conversations can be heard in a number of different ways, the choice of forty reflects the traditional discipline of daily meditation during Lent. Each conversation leads naturally into a brief prayer crafted in the form of a collect.

A number of friends and colleagues have helped me to refine this form of conversation, but my appreciation goes especially to Wyn Evans (now Bishop of St Davids) who brought me to Trinity College Carmarthen and introduced me to the discipline of a daily morning service of the word held in the college chapel for students and for staff. Over a number of years Mole became my trusted companion in accepting a regular turn on the chapel rota.

I am also grateful to the friends and colleagues who have helped to shape this manuscript for me, especially Ann Rees and Diane Drayson, and to David Moloney at Darton, Longman and Todd who remembered a discussion with me in the late 1990s and invited me to translate that discussion into a completed manuscript in time for Lent 2010.

Kenneth Grahame's *The Wind in the Willows* was first published in 1908. A century later I am profoundly grateful to Kenneth Grahame for the stimulation and insight that his work has brought to me and which it continues to bring to me. I am grateful, too, for the way in which Kenneth Grahame's text helps me to see fresh perspectives within the gospel texts on which my faith is grounded and in which my future hope is placed.

# Introduction

It is all too easy for well-known, well-loved passages from the Gospels to grow weary and stale in our minds. From time to time, we need to be shaken from complacency. From time to time, we need to be encouraged to see the Gospel message in a new light and to read familiar passages in a new way. This book has been designed to do just that.

What is often needed to help us see old things in a new way or to read familiar passages in a new light is a conversation partner who asks startling questions, who places ideas side-by-side in an arresting way, and who redirects attention by hinting at unseen connections. In this book, Kenneth Grahame's lovable (and not so lovable) characters are poised to do just that.

In *The Gospel in the Willows* Kenneth Grahame's narrative leads the way and opens the door to deep reflection on forty themes from the gospels. This is not a book to be read quickly or unreflectively. It is a book to be read in sequence, because Kenneth Grahame's narrative needs to be allowed to unfold, but each of the forty gospel themes is self-contained and worth examining in its own right. It would be a mistake to rush on from one chapter to the next.

The idea of selecting forty themes (neither more nor

less) was a deliberate attempt to map onto the traditional forty days of Lent. Here is the time of the liturgical year when Christian disciples are encouraged to deepen their commitment, to refresh their faith, to see old things in a new way, and to read familiar passages of scripture in a new light. In this book, Kenneth Grahame's lovable (and not so lovable) creatures are poised to be our conversation partners and to walk the Lenten path with us.

Of course, it is not just during Lent that it is good to explore new ways of reading scripture, to discover new insights from familiar texts, or to deepen our experience of and commitment to discipleship. In other words, a Lent book is for Life, not just for Lent. I pray that this conversation between *The Wind in the Willows* and the gospel message may prove to be as life-giving to the readers as it has been to the author.

## CHAPTER ONE

# Exploring faith by the river bank

# Episode 1: The call

*Jesus said, 'Come with me.'*

THE RIVER BANK
The mole had been working very hard all the morning, spring-cleaning his little home. First with brooms, then with dusters; then on ladders and steps and chairs, with a brush and a pail of whitewash; till he had dust in his throat and eyes, and splashes of whitewash all over his black fur, and an aching back and weary arms. Spring was moving in the air above and in the earth below and around him, penetrating even his dark and lowly little house with its spirit of divine discontent and longing. It was small wonder, then, that he suddenly flung down his brush on the floor, said 'Bother!' and 'O blow!' and also 'Hang spring-cleaning!' and bolted out of the house without even waiting to put on his coat. Something up above was calling him imperiously, and he made for the steep little tunnel which answered in his case to the gravelled carriage-drive owned by animals whose residences are nearer to the sun and air.

MARK 1:16 – 20, 2:13 – 14
As Jesus walked along the shore of Lake Galilee, he saw two fishermen, Simon and his brother Andrew, catching fish with a net. Jesus said to them, 'Come with me, and I

will teach you to catch men.' At once they left their nets and went with him.

He went a little farther on and saw two other brothers, James and John, the sons of Zebedee. They were in their boat getting their nets ready. As soon as Jesus saw them, he called them; they left their father Zebedee in the boat with the hired men and went with Jesus.

Jesus went back again to the shore of Lake Galilee. A crowd came to him, and he started teaching them. As he walked along, he saw a tax collector, Levi son of Alphaeus, sitting in his office. Jesus said to him, 'Follow me.' Levi got up and followed him.

## MEDITATION

Mole was busy, busy about his business. He was busy with brooms and dusters, on ladders and steps and chairs, with brush and pail and whitewash. Mole was totally active and totally absorbed. Mole was busy, busy until the thread snapped and something, something unaccountable penetrated the innermost springs of his soul.

Simon and Andrew, James and John were busy, busy about their business. They were busy with nets and fishing pots, in boats and shed and market stalls, with the economic forces of supply and demand. Simon and Andrew, James and John were totally active and totally absorbed. Simon and Andrew, James and John were busy, busy until the thread snapped and something, something unaccountable penetrated the innermost springs of their souls.

Levi was busy, busy about his business. He was busy with ledgers and cash, on desks, tables and office counters, with calculators, auditors and work perform-ance indicators. Levi was totally active and totally absorbed. Levi was busy, busy until the thread snapped and something, something unaccountable penetrated the innermost springs of his soul.

Mole had been trapped, trapped in the busyness of his subterranean cavern, trapped until his dark and lowly little house was penetrated with the spirit of divine discontent and longing. Something up above was calling him, calling him imperiously; and he was left with no choice other than to respond.

Simon and Andrew, James and John had been trapped, trapped in the busyness of their lakeside industry, trapped until their dark and lowly little boat was flooded with the spirit of divine discontent and longing. Someone up above was calling them, calling them imperiously; and they were left with no choice other than to respond.

Levi had been trapped, trapped in the busyness of his hated profession, trapped until his dark and lowly little office was illuminated with the spirit of divine discontent and longing. Someone up above was calling him, calling him imperiously; and he was left with no choice other than to respond.

You and I are busy, busy about our business: busy with brooms and dusters; busy with nets and fishing pots; busy with ledgers and cash. You and I are trapped, trapped with the busyness of our own lives. But out there, up above, the spirit of divine discontent is stirring. Let it penetrate your dark and lowly little house. Let it flood your dark and lowly little boat. Let it illuminate your dark and lowly little office. Out there, up above, something is calling, someone is calling. Let that voice penetrate the innermost springs of your soul, until the thread snaps and you are left with no choice other than to respond.

PRAYER
Lord God,
you made us for yourself
and our lives are restless
until they find their rest in you.
Let the spirit of divine discontent stir our souls;
let the voice of divine calling penetrate our minds;
that we may find in you our eternal purpose.
We make our prayer in the name of Jesus.

Amen.

# Episode 2: The teaching

*The people who heard Jesus were
amazed at the way he taught.*

THE RIVER BANK

Mole thought his happiness was complete when, as he
meandered aimlessly along, suddenly he stood by the
edge of a full-fed river. Never in his life had he seen a
river before – this sleek, sinuous, full-bodied animal,
chasing and chuckling, gripping things with a gurgle and
leaving them with a laugh, to fling itself on fresh
playmates that shook themselves free, and were caught
and held again. All was a-shake and a-shiver – glints
and gleams and sparkles, rustle and swirl, chatter and
bubble. The Mole was bewitched, entranced, fascinated.
By the side of the river he trotted as one trots, when
very small, by the side of a man, who holds one
spellbound by exciting stories; and when tired at last,
he sat on the bank, while the river still chattered on to
him, a babbling procession of the best stories in the
world, sent from the heart of the earth to be told at last
to the insatiable sea.

MARK 1:21 – 22, 4:33 – 34

Jesus and his disciples came to the town of Capernaum,
and on the next Sabbath Jesus went to the synagogue and

began to teach. The people who heard him were amazed at the way he taught, for he was not like the teachers of the Law; instead he taught with authority.

Jesus preached his message to the people, using many other parables like these; he told them as much as they could understand. He would not speak to them without using parables, but when he was alone with his disciples, he would explain everything to them.

## MEDITATION

Mole was captivated, spellbound, bewitched, entranced, fascinated. Never in his life had he seen such a river before. Instantly he recognised that the river possessed a self-authenticating authority, an authority all of its own.

The bystanders who heard Jesus speak were captivated, spellbound, bewitched, entranced, fascinated. Never in their lives had they seen such a teacher before. Instantly they recognised that the speaker possessed a self-authenticating authority, an authority all of his own.

Mole was captivated by the sleek, sinuous full-bodied river, with glints and gleams and sparkles, rustle and swirl, chatter and bubble. Mole allowed himself to be led along as the river flowed from place to place, chattering to him, a babbling procession of the best stories in the world, sent from the heart of the earth to be told at last to the insatiable sea.

The bystanders who heard Jesus speak were captivated by the sleek, sinuous, full-bodied teacher, with glints and gleams and sparkles, rustle and swirl, chatter and bubble. The bystanders allowed themselves to be led along as the itinerant teacher flowed from village to village, chattering to them, a babbling procession of the best stories in the world, sent from the heart of heaven to be told at last to the earth's farthest corner.

When at last worn down by the novelty, the intensity, the sheer authority of the river's unceasing voice, Mole sat down by the riverside. In tranquillity Mole could reconstruct the tale and reapply the message to his own developing future.

When at last worn down by the novelty, the intensity, the sheer authority of their itinerant preacher's teaching, the bystanders sat down at the teacher's feet. In tranquillity the bystanders could reconstruct the tale and reapply the message to their own developing futures.

Like Mole, you and I are invited to follow the river that is forever flowing, to follow the river that is forever old, to follow the river that is forever new. Like the bystanders, you and I are invited to follow the itinerant teacher who is ever flowing, to follow the words of teaching that are forever old, to follow the words of teaching that are forever new.

Like Mole, you and I are invited to surrender ourselves, captivated, spellbound, bewitched, entranced and fascinated. Like the bystanders, you and I are invited to judge for ourselves the self-authenticating authority of Jesus the teacher. And like them, we are invited to unravel the hidden parable, to unlock the secret of the Kingdom, and to be transformed by the boundless mystery, as we follow the voice of the teacher flowing through time, and into eternity.

PRAYER
Lord Jesus Christ,
your words give life.
Open our ears to your teaching;
open our hearts to your message;
open our lives to your prompting;
that we may recognise your authority
and dedicate ourselves to your service.
We make our prayer in your name.

Amen.

# Episode 3: The crossing

*Jesus said, 'Let us go across
to the other side of the lake.'*

THE RIVER BANK

Then the two animals stood and regarded each other
cautiously.

'Hullo, Mole!' said the Water Rat.

'Hullo, Rat!' said the Mole.

'Would you like to come over?' inquired the Rat
presently.

'Oh, it's all very well to *talk*,' said the Mole, rather
pettishly, he being new to a river and riverside life and its
ways.

The Rat said nothing, but stooped and unfastened a
rope and hauled on it; then lightly stepped into a little boat
which the Mole had not observed. It was painted blue
outside and white within, and was just the size for two
animals; and the Mole's whole heart went out to it at once,
even though he did not yet fully understand its uses.

The Rat sculled smartly across and made fast. Then
he held up his fore-paw as the Mole stepped gingerly
down.

'Lean on that!' he said. 'Now then, step lively!' and
the Mole to his surprise and rapture found himself
actually seated in the stern of a real boat.

MARK 4:35 – 41

On the evening of that same day Jesus said to his disciples, 'Let us go across to the other side of the lake.' So they left the crowd; the disciples got into the boat in which Jesus was already sitting, and they took him with them. Other boats were there too. Suddenly a strong wind blew up, and the waves began to spill over into the boat, so that it was about to fill with water. Jesus was in the back of the boat, sleeping with his head on a pillow. The disciples woke him up and said, 'Teacher, don't you care that we are about to die?'

Jesus stood up and commanded the wind, 'Be quiet!' and he said to the waves, 'Be still!' The wind died down, and there was a great calm. Then Jesus said to his disciples, 'Why are you frightened? Have you still no faith?'

But they were terribly afraid and said to one another, 'Who is this man? Even the wind and the waves obey him!'

MEDITATION

Standing there on the river's edge, Mole knew that he was standing on the edge of a tremendous new experience. Mole had heard the call of the river, and he had responded to that call. Mole had listened to the tales of the river, sent from the heart of the earth, and he was being transformed by their message. Mole had witnessed the power of the river, and he was being attracted by its self-authenticating authority. But, as yet, Mole had not entrusted himself to the river.

Standing there on the edge of their commitment to Jesus, the disciples knew that they were standing on the edge of a tremendous new experience. The disciples had heard the call of the teacher, and they had responded to that call. The disciples had listened to the tales of the teacher, sent from the heart of heaven, and they were being transformed by his message. The disciples had witnessed the healing power of the teacher, and were being attracted by his self-authenticating authority. But, as yet, the disciples had not entrusted themselves to the teacher.

Standing there on the river's edge, Mole knew that he had to step out in faith, step out into the unknown. A distant voice was inviting him to leave the safety of the dry land, to leave the bank on which all his experience had been based, and to put his trust in an unknown boat.

Standing there on the edge of their commitment to Jesus, the disciples knew that they had to step out in faith, step out into the unknown. A distant voice was inviting them to leave the safety of the dry land, to leave the shore on which all their experience had been based, and to put their trust in an unknown vessel.

Leaving terra firma firmly behind, Mole stretched out his paw and found Rat's firm confident grasp. 'Lean on that,' said Rat, and Mole, to his surprise and rapture, found himself actually seated safe in the stern of the boat. At last Mole could rest his faith on first-paw experience. Having allowed his very wellbeing to be threatened, Mole could for himself experience that salvation, that healing and that safety in which real conversion is grounded.

Leaving terra firma firmly behind, the disciples stretched out their hands and found Jesus' firm confident grasp. 'Be quiet, be still, have faith,' said Jesus, and the disciples to their surprise and rapture, found themselves actually seated safe in the boat with Jesus, too, on board. At last the disciples could rest their faith on first-hand experience. Having allowed their very wellbeing to be threatened, the disciples could for themselves experience that salvation, that healing and that safety in which real conversion is grounded.

Like Mole, you and I have heard the call of the river, that goes on flowing through all eternity, and we have responded to that call. Like the disciples, we have listened to the tales of the teacher, sent from the heart of heaven, and we are being transformed by their message. Now we, like them, must grasp the hand that has been held out to us. We must leave behind the security of terra firma and learn for real the lesson of setting out on the sea of faith. Jesus calls us to cross over to the other side of the lake and to trust him for the journey. Allowing our very wellbeing to be threatened on the sea of faith, allows us also to experience for ourselves that salvation, that healing and that safety in which real conversion is grounded.

PRAYER
Lord Jesus Christ,
you call your followers
to leave their old selves behind
and to trust to you their future lives.
Hold out your hand to us
and give us courage to grasp hold of you;
that we may experience your transforming love.
We make our prayer in your name.

Amen.

# Episode 4: The feeding

*The disciples had only one loaf
with them in the boat.*

THE RIVER BANK

'Look here!' said the Rat. 'If you've really nothing else on hand this morning, supposing we drop down the river together, and have a long day of it?'

The Mole waggled his toes from sheer happiness, spread his chest with a sigh of full contentment, and leaned back blissfully into the soft cushions. '*What* a day I'm having!' he said. 'Let us start at once!'

'Hold hard a minute, then!' said the Rat. He looped the painter through a ring in his landing-stage, climbed up into his hole above, and after a short interval reappeared staggering under a fat, wicker luncheon-basket.

'Shove that under your feet,' he observed to the Mole, as he passed it down into the boat. Then he untied the painter and took the sculls again.

'What's inside it?' asked the Mole, wriggling with curiosity.

'There's cold chicken inside it,' replied the Rat briefly; 'coldtonguecoldhamcoldbeefpickledgherkinssalad-frenchrollscresssandwidgespottedmeatgingerbeerlemon-adesodawater –'

'O stop, stop,' cried the Mole in ecstasies: 'This is too much!'

'Do you really think so?' inquired the Rat seriously. 'It's only what I always take on these little excursions; and the other animals are always telling me that I'm a mean beast and cut it *very* fine!'

## MARK 8:14 – 21

The disciples had forgotten to bring enough bread and had only one loaf with them in the boat. 'Take care,' Jesus warned them, 'and be on your guard against the yeast of the Pharisees and the yeast of Herod.'

They started discussing among themselves: 'He says this because we haven't any bread.'

Jesus knew what they were saying, so he asked them, 'Why are you discussing about not having any bread? Don't you know or understand yet? Are your minds so dull? You have eyes – can't you see? You have ears – can't you hear? Don't you remember when I broke the five loaves for the five thousand people? How many baskets full of leftover pieces did you take up?'

'Twelve,' they answered.

'And when I broke the seven loaves for the four thousand people,' asked Jesus, 'how many baskets full of leftover pieces did you take up?'

'Seven,' they answered.

'And you still don't understand?' he asked them.

## MEDITATION

Some travellers travel more lightly than others. When Rat travels, he travels with cold chicken, cold tongue, cold beef, pickled gherkins, salad, french rolls, cress sandwiches, potted meat, ginger beer, lemonade and soda water. Even then the other animals are always telling him that he is a mean beast and that he is cutting it *very* fine.

Some travellers travel more lightly than others. When the twelve disciples travel, then they indeed cut it *very* fine. They bring but one loaf, and what is one loaf among twelve disciples and their master?

Ardent travellers are always prepared, ready to undertake a new journey at the drop of a hat. Rat, it seems, is always prepared for travel. The luncheon-basket is ready packed at hand, full to the brim with cold chicken, cold tongue, cold beef, pickled gherkins, salad, french rolls, cress sandwiches, potted meat, ginger beer, lemonade and soda water.

Ardent travellers are always prepared, ready to undertake a new journey at the drop of a hat. The twelve disciples, it seems, are always prepared for the missionary journey to which they are called. The luncheon basket is ready packed at hand with the one solitary loaf. It is true that they cut it *very* fine, but then one loaf *is* adequate in the hands of their leader.

Imagine what Rat can do when he comes to unpack the luncheon basket, full with cold chicken, cold tongue, cold beef, pickled gherkins, salad, french rolls, cress sandwiches, potted meat, ginger beer, lemonade and soda water. Yet even then the other animals are always telling him that he is a mean beast who cuts it *very* fine.

Imagine what Jesus can do when he comes to unpack the luncheon basket, full with five loaves. The people of Israel were fed and twelve baskets were filled with the leftovers. This Jesus is no mean beast.

Imagine what Jesus can do when he comes to unpack the luncheon basket, full with seven loaves. The whole of the Gentile world was fed and seven baskets were filled with the leftovers. This Jesus is no mean beast.

Imagine what Jesus can do when he comes to unpack the luncheon basket, full with one loaf, in the upper room. The whole of the human race is invited to feed on him who is the Living Bread. This Jesus is no mean beast.

Imagine what Jesus can do when he comes to unpack the luncheon basket, full with one loaf, on the Emmaus road. The two travellers identify their risen Lord and know him in the breaking of bread. This Jesus is no mean beast.

Like Rat, you and I are invited to stand prepared for those journeys on which Christ wishes to send his Church. Be ready, then, with the loaf of the Kingdom packed in your luncheon basket, and remember the power of that loaf in the hands of your master.

PRAYER
Lord Jesus Christ,
you promise to be with your people
throughout the journey of life.
Travel with us on our way
and make yourself known to us
in the breaking of bread.
We make our prayer in your name.

Amen.

# Episode 5:
# The apprenticeship

*Peter said, 'Lord, order me to come
out on the water to you.'*

## THE RIVER BANK

The afternoon sun was getting low as the Rat sculled gently homewards in a dreamy mood, murmuring poetry-things over to himself, and not paying much attention to Mole. But the Mole was very full of lunch, and self-satisfaction, and pride, and already quite at home in a boat (so he thought) and was getting a bit restless besides: and presently he said, 'Ratty! Please, *I* want to row, now!'

The Rat shook his head with a smile. 'Not yet, my young friend,' he said – 'wait till you've had a few lessons. It's not so easy as it looks.'

The Mole was quiet for a minute or two. But he began to feel more and more jealous of Rat, sculling so strongly and so easily along, and his pride began to whisper that he could do it every bit as well. He jumped up and seized the sculls, so suddenly, that the Rat, who was gazing out over the water and saying more poetry-things to himself, was taken by surprise and fell backwards off his seat with his legs in the air for the second time, while the triumphant Mole took his place and grabbed the sculls with entire confidence.

'Stop it, you *silly* ass!' cried the Rat, from the bottom of the boat. 'You can't do it! You'll have us over!'

The Mole flung his sculls back with a flourish, and made a great dig at the water. He missed the surface altogether, his legs flew up above his head, and he found himself lying on the top of the prostrate Rat. Greatly alarmed, he made a grab at the side of the boat, and the next moment – Sploosh!

Over went the boat, and he found himself struggling in the river.

## MATTHEW 14:22 – 32

Then Jesus made the disciples get into the boat and go on ahead to the other side of the lake, while he sent the people away. After sending the people away, he went up a hill by himself to pray. When evening came, Jesus was there alone; and by this time the boat was far out in the lake, tossed about by the waves, because the wind was blowing against it.

Between three and six o'clock in the morning Jesus came to the disciples, walking on the water. When they saw him walking on the water, they were terrified. 'It's a ghost!' they said, and screamed with fear.

Jesus spoke to them at once. 'Courage!' he said. 'It is I. Don't be afraid!'

Then Peter spoke up. 'Lord, if it is really you, order me to come out on the water to you.'

'Come!' answered Jesus. So Peter got out of the boat and started walking on the water to Jesus. But when he noticed the strong wind, he was afraid and started to sink down in the water.

'Save me, Lord!' he cried.

At once Jesus reached out and grabbed hold of him

and said, 'How little faith you have! Why did you doubt?'

They both got into the boat, and the wind died down. Then the disciples in the boat worshipped Jesus. 'Truly you are the Son of God!' they exclaimed.

## MEDITATION

Mole had come a long, long way since he first met Rat. He was a changed creature, learning a new way of life, a new set of priorities, and a new image of his own potential. A good disciple, Mole was eager to learn and eager to excel. His apprenticeship was very well under way. 'Ratty!' he said, '*I* want to row, now!'

Peter had come a long, long way since he first met Jesus. He was a changed man, learning a new way of life, a new set of priorities, and a new image of his own potential. A good disciple, Peter was eager to learn and eager to excel. His apprenticeship was well under way. 'Jesus!' he said, '*I* want to walk on the water, now!'

Ratty acted as a sensitive and protective guardian for his young disciple. Rat shook his head with a smile. 'Not yet, my young friend,' he said, 'wait till you've had a few lessons. It's not so easy as it looks.'

Jesus did not act as such a sensitive and protective guardian for his young disciple. Jesus nodded his head with a smile, knowing full well the consequences of his invitation. 'Come!' answered Jesus, 'It's as easy as it looks!'

Ratty's warning went unheeded. Mole whispered to himself that he could do it every bit as well. He grabbed the sculls with entire confidence and made a great dig at the water. And the next moment – Sploosh! Over went the boat, and Mole found himself struggling in the river.

Jesus' invitation was heeded instantly. Peter whispered

to himself that he could do it every bit as well. He got out of the boat with entire confidence and started walking on the water to Jesus. And the next moment – Sploosh! Peter found himself sinking down in the water.

When the boat went over, Ratty was powerless to assist his struggling disciple. Indeed, rescuing capsized Moles is not so easy as it looks.

When Peter went down in the water, Jesus stood firm and came instantly to his aid. Indeed, rescuing sinking apostles is a great deal easier than it looks.

Like Peter, you and I are called by Jesus to follow his example. We are called as disciples to observe our master closely and to emulate all that he does well. Listen carefully to his invitation and trust him when he calls. By responding to his call you will learn how realistic you are in your response. But you can do so in the firm confidence that he who calls will not permit you to sink.

PRAYER
Lord Jesus,
you call your followers to step out in faith.
Help us to hear your call
and to trust your calling,
for you are our God
now and for ever.

Amen.

## CHAPTER TWO

# Learning to be disciples on the open road

# Episode 6: Asking favours

*Jesus said, 'You don't know what you
are asking for.'*

THE OPEN ROAD

'Ratty,' said the Mole suddenly, one bright summer morning, 'if you please, I want to ask you a favour.'

The Rat was sitting on the river bank, singing a little song. He had just composed it himself, so he was very taken up with it, and would not pay proper attention to Mole or anything else. ...

'I don't know that I think so *very* much of that little song, Rat,' observed the Mole cautiously. He was no poet himself and didn't care who knew it; and he had a candid nature.... .

'But what I wanted to ask you was, won't you take me to call on Mr Toad? I've heard so much about him, and I do so want to make his acquaintance.'

'Why, certainly,' said the good-natured Rat, jumping to his feet and dismissing poetry from his mind for the day. 'Get the boat out, and we'll paddle up there at once. It's never the wrong time to call on Toad.'

MARK 10:35 – 40

Then James and John, the sons of Zebedee, came to Jesus.

'Teacher,' they said, 'there is something we want you to do for us.'

'What is it?' Jesus asked them.

They answered, 'When you sit on your throne in your glorious Kingdom, we want you to let us sit with you, one at your right and one at your left.'

Jesus said to them, 'You don't know what you are asking for. Can you drink the cup of suffering that I must drink? Can you be baptized in the way I must be baptized?'

'We can,' they answered.

Jesus said to them, 'You will indeed drink the cup I must drink and be baptized in the way I must be baptized. But I do not have the right to choose who will sit at my right and my left. It is God who will give these places to those for whom he has prepared them.'

## MEDITATION

'If you please,' said the Mole suddenly, 'I want to ask you a favour.' And the Rat just went on singing, singing a little song. 'If you please,' said the brothers, James and John, suddenly, 'I want to ask you a favour.' And Jesus just went on singing, singing the song of pilgrimage.

The Mole had rowed in the same boat as the Rat long enough and well enough to dare to pose the question. And the Rat just went on singing, singing a little song. The brothers, James and John, had rowed in the same boat as Jesus long enough and well enough to dare to pose the question. And Jesus just went on singing, singing the song of pilgrimage.

It was, after all, a calculated risk. The Mole was putting his confidence in the Rat's friendship right there on the line. And the Rat just went on singing, singing a little song. It was, after all, a calculated risk. The brothers, James and John, were putting their confidence in Jesus' friendship right there on the line. And Jesus just went on singing, singing the song of pilgrimage.

The Rat could have closed down the conversation there and then, then and there. The Rat could just have gone on singing, singing a little song. But the Rat gave the invitation; the Rat made the opening. 'What is it?' the Rat asked. Jesus could have closed down the conversation there and then, then and there. Jesus could just have gone on singing, singing the song of pilgrimage. But Jesus gave the invitation; Jesus made the opening. 'What is it?' Jesus asked.

The door was open and the way was clear. 'But what I wanted to ask you was this,' blurted out the Mole. 'Won't you take me to call on Mr Toad?' The door was open and the way was clear. 'But what I wanted to ask you was this,' blurted out the two brothers, James and John. 'Won't you take us to sit with you, when you reign in your Kingdom, one on your right hand and one on your left hand?'

The Rat's little song had been interrupted. The request had been made. 'Why, certainly,' said the good-natured Rat, jumping to his feet and dismissing poetry from his mind for the day. But deep down inside the Rat knew that his impetuous companion needed protecting from himself and from the Toad. And the Rat murmured to himself in a low voice, 'You don't know what you are asking for. You don't know what you are letting yourself in for.'

Jesus' song of pilgrimage had been interrupted. The request had been made. 'You don't know what you are asking for. You don't know what you are letting yourself in for,' said the good-natured Jesus, jumping to his feet and protecting his impetuous disciples. But deep down inside Jesus knew that his impetuous companions were deeply committed to his cause. Jesus murmured to himself in a low voice, 'Why, certainly. You shall share my glory, but first you must share my sufferings.'

Be bold, then. Summon up the courage to interrupt the song and to ask the question that leads to life. But, first, accept the truth that the invitation is to share the Messiah's suffering before sharing the glory.

PRAYER
Lord Jesus Christ,
you listened to your disciples' questions.
Give us the courage to ask,
the wisdom to understand what we ask
and the patience to accept your answer.
We make our prayer
in your name.

Amen.

# Episode 7:
# Affirming the past

*Jesus said, 'Anyone who starts to plough and then keeps looking back is of no use to the Kingdom of God.'*

THE OPEN ROAD

'O, pooh! boating!' interrupted the Toad, in great disgust. 'Silly boyish amusement. I've given that up *long* ago. Sheer waste of time, that's what it is. It makes me downright sorry to see you fellows, who ought to know better, spending all your energies in that aimless manner. No, I've discovered the real thing, the only genuine occupation for a lifetime. I propose to devote the remainder of mine to it, and can only regret the wasted years that lie behind me squandered in trivialities. Come with me, dear Ratty, and your amiable friend also, if he will be so very good, just as far as the stable-yard, and you shall see what you shall see!'

He led the way to the stable-yard accordingly, the Rat following with a most mistrustful expression; and there, drawn out of the coach-house into the open, they saw a gipsy caravan, shining with newness, painted a canary-yellow picked out with green, and red wheels.

LUKE 9:57 – 62

As they went on their way, a man said to Jesus, 'I will follow you wherever you go.'

Jesus said to him, 'Foxes have holes, and birds have nests, but the Son of Man has nowhere to lie down and rest.'

He said to another man, 'Follow me.' But that man said, 'Sir, first let me go back and bury my father.'

Jesus answered, 'Let the dead bury their own dead. You go and proclaim the Kingdom of God.'

Another man said, 'I will follow you, sir; but first let me go and say good-bye to my family.'

Jesus said to him, 'Anyone who starts to plough and then keeps looking back is of no use to the Kingdom of God.'

MEDITATION

The Toad has his vision fixed firmly on the road ahead. Yesterday it may well have been boating; but today all that is pushed firmly into the past. 'O, pooh! boating!' interrupted the Toad, in great disgust. 'Silly boyish amusement. I've given that up *long* ago.' Today's the day. Today's the day of the gipsy caravan, shining with newness, painted a canary-yellow picked out with green, and red wheels. The Toad had his vision fixed firmly on the road ahead.

The would-be disciple has his vision fixed firmly on the road behind. Tomorrow may well be listening and learning, healing and casting out demons, following and obeying the master. But today all that is pushed firmly into the future. 'First let me go back,' interrupted the would-be disciple. 'First let me go back and bury my father.' Tomorrow is the day. Tomorrow is the day of the gipsy caravan, shining with newness, painted a canary-yellow picked out with green, and red wheels. The would-be disciple has his vision fixed firmly on the road behind.

The Toad is so concerned with the future that he forgets the past. The old life of boating is relegated to boyhood amusement. The lessons of boating are left in yesterday's world, too distant from the concerns of today to be allowed to influence the shape of tomorrow. 'Sheer waste of time, that's what it is,' interrupted the Toad. Toad is so concerned with the future that he forgets the past.

The would-be disciple is so concerned with the past that he has no grasp on the future. The new life of listening and learning, healing and casting out demons, following and obeying the master is allocated to some distant future. The lessons of discipleship are projected into tomorrow's world, too distant from the concerns of today to be influenced by the shape of the past. 'Let me first go and say goodbye to my family,' interrupted the would-be disciple. The would-be disciple is so concerned with the past that he has no grasp of the future.

Had the Toad listened to the lessons learnt in boating, he would have driven his caravan, shining with newness, painted a canary-yellow picked out with green, on a much steadier course. Had the Toad listened to lessons learnt in the past he could have predicted and begun to shape his responses in the future. But the Toad has his vision too firmly fixed on the road ahead.

Had the would-be disciple opened his mind to the lessons yet to be learnt in the path of discipleship, he would have viewed his commitment to serving his father until his father's death in a completely different light. Had the would-be disciple opened his mind to the lessons yet to be learnt in the future, he could have predicted how new life could have been proclaimed to his father as well. But the would-be disciple had his vision too firmly fixed on the road behind.

Pray, then, that unlike the Toad, and unlike the would-be disciple, we may have the confidence to look both to the road ahead and to the road behind.

PRAYER
Lord Jesus Christ,
you call your followers to a new beginning.
Help us to hear your call,
and to set our sight on the future,
without losing sight of the past.
We make our prayer in the name of Jesus.

Amen.

# Episode 8:
# Finding real life

*Simon Peter said, 'You have the words
that give eternal life.'*

THE OPEN ROAD

'There you are!' cried the Toad, straddling and expanding himself. 'There's real life for you, embodied in that little cart. The open road, the dusty highway, the heath, the common, the hedgerows, the rolling downs! Camps, villages, towns, cities! Here to-day, up and off to somewhere else to-morrow! Travel, change, interest, excitement! The whole world before you, and a horizon that's always changing! And mind, this is the very finest cart of its sort that was ever built, without any exception. Come inside and look at the arrangements. Planned 'em all myself, I did!'

The Mole was tremendously interested and excited, and followed him eagerly up the steps and into the interior of the caravan. The Rat only snorted and thrust his hands deep into his pockets, remaining where he was.

It was indeed very compact and comfortable. Little sleeping-bunks – a little table that folded up against the wall – a cooking-stove, lockers, bookshelves, a bird cage with a bird in it; and pots, pans, jugs and kettles of every size and variety.

'All complete!' said the Toad triumphantly, pulling open a locker. 'You see – biscuits, potted lobster, sardines – everything you can possibly want. Soda-water here – baccy there – letter-paper, bacon, jam, cards and dominoes – you'll find,' he continued, as they descended the steps again, 'you'll find that nothing whatever has been forgotten, when we make our start this afternoon.'

JOHN 6:60 – 68

Many of his followers heard this and said, 'This teaching is too hard. Who can listen to it?'

Without being told, Jesus knew that they were grumbling about this, so he said to them, 'Does this make you want to give up? Suppose, then, that you should see the Son of Man go back up to the place where he was before? What gives life is God's Spirit; man's power is of no use at all. The words I have spoken to you bring God's life-giving Spirit. Yet some of you do not believe.' (Jesus knew from the very beginning who were the ones that would not believe and which one would betray him.) And he added, 'This is the very reason I told you that no one can come to me unless the Father makes it possible for him to do so.'

Because of this, many of Jesus' followers turned back and would not go with him any more. So he asked the twelve disciples, 'And you – would you also like to leave?'

Simon Peter answered him, 'Lord, to whom would we go? You have the words that give eternal life.'

MEDITATION

'There you are!' cried the Toad. 'There's real life for you.' And the Toad was looking at the little cart.

The Toad saw right through the little cart, shining with newness, painted in a canary-yellow picked out with green, and red wheels. The Toad saw right through the little cart into the great space beyond. The cart was a mere symbol, a mere sacrament that focused more than could be put into words, more than could be expressed through thought, more than could be captured in picture.

The Toad saw right through the little cart. Beyond the little cart he saw the open road, the dusty highway, the heath, the common, the hedgerows, the rolling downs! Camps, villages, towns, cities! Like a sacrament, the little cart focused the Toad's attention and directed him to the heart of reality and to the secret of life itself. 'There you are!' cried the Toad. 'There's real life for you.' And the Toad was looking at the little cart.

'There you are!' cried Simon Peter. 'There's real life for you.' And Simon Peter was looking at the little peripatetic preacher.

Simon Peter saw right through the little preacher, dusty from the road, weary from the journey and worn down by their lack of faith. Simon Peter saw right through the little preacher into the great space beyond. The preacher was a mere symbol, a mere sacrament that focused more than could be put into words, more than could be expressed through thought, more than could be captured in picture.

Simon Peter saw right through the little preacher. Beyond the little preacher he experienced the life-giving healings, he heard the life-giving teachings, he participated in the life-giving feedings. Like a sacrament, the little preacher focused Simon Peter's attention and directed him to the heart of reality and to the secret of life itself. 'There you are!' cried Simon Peter. 'There's real life for you.' And Simon Peter was looking at the little peripatetic preacher.

You and I, too, are invited to experience the power of sacramental focus. See the little cart, and begin to smell the open road. Meet the little peripatetic preacher, and begin to witness the life-shaping teaching, the life-giving healing, the life-supporting feeding. Hear the word of scripture proclaimed and be confronted by the word of life. Break open the loaf of eucharistic bread and be transformed by the body of Christ. 'There you are!' cried the Toad. 'There you are!' cried Simon Peter. 'There's real life for you!'

PRAYER
Lord Jesus Christ,
you open the eyes of your followers.
Open our ears to the word of life.
Open our mouths to the bread of life.
Open our hearts to you, the Lord of life.
For you are our God,
now and for ever.

Amen.

# Episode 9: Shaking the dust

*Jesus said, 'Shake the dust off your feet.'*

THE OPEN ROAD

When they were quite ready, the now triumphant Toad led his companions to the paddock and set them to capture the old grey horse, who, without having been consulted, and to his own extreme annoyance, had been told off by Toad for the dustiest job in this dusty expedition. He frankly preferred the paddock, and took a deal of catching. Meantime Toad packed the lockers still tighter with necessaries, and hung nose-bags, nets of onions, bundles of hay, and baskets from the bottom of the cart. At last the horse was caught and harnessed, and they set off, all talking at once, each animal either trudging by the side of the cart or sitting on the shaft, as the humour took him. It was a golden afternoon. The smell of the dust they kicked up was rich and satisfying; out of thick orchards on either side the road, birds called and whistled to them cheerily; good-natured wayfarers, passing them, gave them 'Good day', or stopped to say nice things about their beautiful cart; and rabbits, sitting at their front doors in the hedgerows, held up their fore-paws, and said, 'O my! O my! O my!'

MARK 6:6 – 11

Then Jesus went to the villages round there, teaching the people. He called the twelve disciples together and sent them out two by two. He gave them authority over the evil spirits and ordered them, 'Don't take anything with you on your journey except a stick – no bread, no beggar's bag, no money in your pockets. Wear sandals, but don't carry an extra shirt.' He also said, 'Wherever you are welcomed, stay in the same house until you leave that place. If you come to a town where people do not welcome you or will not listen to you, leave it and shake the dust off your feet. That will be a warning to them!'

MEDITATION

Pulling the gipsy caravan is a dusty old job, no matter how brightly the sides are painted. Out there on the open road, long before the days of tarmac, dust was the number one enemy of the old grey horse, greying still with the ingrained dust kicked high by the worn-down hooves. Pulling the gipsy caravan is a dusty old job, no matter how brightly the sides are painted.

For the Mole, for the Rat, for the Toad, sitting there, high on the gipsy caravan, the smell of the dust they kicked up was rich and satisfying. It spoke to them clearly of the kind of country through which they were passing. It spoke to them clearly of the kind of people among whom they were moving. And at the end of the day the dust would hang, clinging on clothes and in fur, repeating the tale of the day's best experiences. For the Mole, for the Rat, for the Toad, sitting there, high on the gipsy caravan, the smell of the dust they kicked up was rich and satisfying.

At the end of the day for the old grey horse, when the

travelling was done and the caravan rested, the dust remained. The taste of the dust in the mouth, the smell of the dust in the nostrils, the texture of the dust in the hoofs, the sight of the dust on the mane, all reminded the old grey horse that no one consulted him when he was assigned for the dustiest job in this dusty expedition. At the end of the day, for the old grey horse, when the travelling was done and the caravan rested, the dust remained. No wonder, then, the old grey horse shook the dust from off his feet.

Bringing the gospel to far-spread towns is a dusty old job, no matter how brightly the towns are painted. Out there on the open road, long before the days of tarmac, dust was the number one enemy of the old grey preachers, greying still with the ingrained dust kicked high by the worn-down sandal. Bringing the gospel to far-spread towns is a dusty old job, no matter how brightly the towns are painted.

For Peter, for James, for John, riding there high on the good news of the gospel, the smell of the dust they kicked up was rich and satisfying. It spoke to them clearly of the kind of country through which they were passing. It spoke to them clearly of the kind of people among whom they were moving. And at the end of the day, the dust would hang, clinging on clothes and in hair, repeating the tale of the day's best experiences. For Peter, for James, for John, riding there high on the good news of the gospel, the smell of the dust they kicked up was rich and satisfying.

At the end of the day for Peter, for James, for John, when the preaching was done and the gospel rested, the dust remained. The taste of the dust in the mouth, the smell of the dust in the nostrils, the texture of the dust in the sandals, the sight of the dust on the clothes, all reminded them of the invitation rejected, the preaching unheeded, the gospel spurned, and the goodwill unreciprocated. At the end of the day for Peter, for James, for John, when the preaching was done and the gospel rested, the dust remained. No wonder, then, that Jesus himself advises them to shake the dust from off their feet, whensoever and wheresoever that dust speaks to them of the rejection of their Lord and master.

PRAYER
Lord Jesus Christ,
you send your followers
to bring your good news to all people.
Send us out in your name
and equip our feet for the journeys
undertaken to proclaim the gospel of peace.
For you are our God,
now and always.

Amen.

# Episode 10: Meal time

*Jesus said, 'Come and eat.'*

THE OPEN ROAD
Late in the evening, tired and happy and miles from
home, they drew up on a remote common far from
habitations, turned the horse loose to graze, and ate their
simple supper sitting on the grass by the side of the cart.
Toad talked big about all he was going to do in the days
to come, while stars grew fuller and larger all around
them, and a yellow moon, appearing suddenly and silently
from nowhere in particular, came to keep them company
and listen to their talk. At last they turned into their little
bunks in the cart; and Toad, kicking out his legs, sleepily
said, 'Well, good night, you fellows! This is the real life for
a gentleman!'

JOHN 21:3 – 12A
Simon Peter said to the others, 'I am going fishing.'

'We will come with you,' they told him. So they went
out in a boat, but all that night they did not catch a thing.
As the sun was rising, Jesus stood at the water's edge, but
the disciples did not know that it was Jesus. Then he
asked them, 'Young men, haven't you caught anything?'

'Not a thing,' they answered.

He said to them, 'Throw your net out on the right side

of the boat, and you will catch some.' So they threw the net out and could not pull it back in, because they had caught so many fish.

The disciple whom Jesus loved said to Peter, 'It is the Lord!' When Peter heard that it was the Lord he wrapped his outer garment round him (for he had taken his clothes off) and jumped into the water. The other disciples came to shore in the boat, pulling the net full of fish. They were not very far from land, about a hundred metres away. When they stepped ashore, there was a charcoal fire there with fish on it and some bread. Then Jesus said to them, 'Bring some of the fish you have just caught.'

Simon Peter went aboard and dragged the net ashore full of big fish, a hundred and fifty-three in all; even though there were so many, still the net did not tear. Jesus said to them, 'Come and eat.'

MEDITATION

It was late, late, late in the day. The Rat, the Toad and the Mole were tired, tired, tired. They had travelled all day in the gipsy caravan, shining with newness, painted a canary-yellow picked out with green, and red wheels. They had travelled all day and travelling is a wearisome matter.

It was late, late, late in the day. The Rat, the Toad and the Mole were the happiest of creatures, the happiest of creatures. They had travelled all day and caught the richest of experiences, the richest of experiences. Contentment coloured their tiredness.

It was late, late, late in the day. The Rat, the Toad and the Mole drew up towards a remote common far from habitations, far from habitations. And suddenly their thoughts turned to supper. It was late, late, late in the day.

It was early, early, early in the day. Peter, James and John were tired, tired, tired. They had fished all night in the little boat, shining with newness, painted a canary-yellow picked out with green, and red oars. They had fished all night and fishing is a wearisome matter.

It was early, early, early in the day. Peter, James and John were the unhappiest of creatures, the unhappiest of creatures. They had fished all night and caught the poorest of catches, the poorest of catches. Discontent coloured their tiredness.

It was early, early, early in the day. Peter, James and John rowed towards a remote shore far from habitation, far from habitation. And suddenly their thoughts turned to breakfast. It was late, late, late in the day.

The Rat, the Toad and the Mole were hungry, hungry, hungry, as they drew up towards a remote common far from habitation. And when the yellow moon, appearing suddenly and silently from nowhere in particular, came to keep them company and listen to their talk, they knew their store cupboards to be well packed and their larder to be full.

The Rat, the Toad and the Mole were hungry, hungry, hungry, as the yellow moon, appearing suddenly and silently from nowhere in particular, came to keep them company, listen to their talk, and invite them to share supper. 'Come and eat,' said the yellow moon. And the Rat, the Toad and the Mole did eat. It was late, late, late. And the Rat, the Toad and the Mole were fed, fed to their contentment. Thanks be to God!

Peter, James and John were hungry, hungry, hungry, as they rowed towards a remote shore far from habitation. And when the stranger on the shore, appearing suddenly and silently from nowhere in particular, came to keep them company and listen to their talk, they knew their nets to be empty and their larder to be bare.

Peter, James and John were hungry, hungry, hungry, as the stranger on the shore, appearing suddenly and silently from nowhere in particular, came to keep them company, listen to their talk, and invite them to share breakfast. 'Come and eat,' said the stranger on the shore. And Peter, James and John did eat. It was early, early, early. And Peter, James and John were fed, fed to their contentment. Thanks be to God!

PRAYER
Lord Jesus Christ,
you call your followers to feast at your table.
Feed our bodies on the living bread.
Feed our minds on the living word.
Feed our souls to eternal life.
We make our prayer
in your name.

Amen.

## CHAPTER THREE

# Hearing parables in the Wild Wood

# Episode 11:
# Observing people

*Scripture says, 'We played wedding music for you, but you wouldn't dance!'*

THE WILD WOOD

The Mole had long wanted to make the acquaintance of the Badger. He seemed, by all accounts, to be such an important personage and, though rarely visible, to make his unseen influence felt by everybody about the place. But whenever the Mole mentioned his wish to the Water Rat he always found himself put off. 'It's alright,' the Rat would say. 'Badger'll turn up some day or other – he's always turning up – and then I'll introduce you. The best of fellows! But you must not only take him *as* you find him, but *when* you find him.'

'Couldn't you ask him here – dinner or something?' said the Mole.

'He wouldn't come,' replied the Rat simply. 'Badger hates Society, and invitations, and dinner, and all that sort of thing.'

'Well, then, supposing we go and call on *him*?' suggested the Mole.

'O, I'm sure he wouldn't like that at *all*,' said the Rat,

quite alarmed. 'He's so very shy, he'd be sure to be offended.'

LUKE 7:31 – 35

Jesus continued, 'Now to what can I compare the people of this day? What are they like? They are like children sitting in the market-place. One group shouts to the other, "We played wedding music for you, but you wouldn't dance! We sang funeral songs, but you wouldn't cry!" John the Baptist came, and he fasted and drank no wine, and you said, "He has a demon in him!" The Son of Man came, and he ate and drank, and you said, "Look at this man! He is a glutton and a drinker, a friend of tax collectors and other outcasts!" God's wisdom, however, is shown to be true by all who accept it.'

MEDITATION

The Badger is an awfully unsociable fellow. The Badger hates society. The Badger hates invitations. The Badger hates dinners. The Badger hates all that sort of thing. The Badger is an awfully unsociable fellow.

The Badger's friends find it awfully difficult to know how to take him. They played wedding music for the Badger, but the Badger wouldn't dance. They threw a party for the Badger, but the Badger wouldn't come. The Badger's friends find it awfully difficult to know how to take him.

And yet, by all accounts, the Badger seems to be such an important personage. By all accounts, though rarely visible, the Badger seems to make his unseen influence felt by everybody about the place. I wonder why that is so?

The Baptist is an awfully unsociable fellow. The Baptist hates society. The Baptist hates invitations. The

Baptist hates dinners. The Baptist hates all that sort of thing. The Baptist is an awfully unsociable fellow.

The Baptist's friends find it awfully difficult to know how to take him. They played wedding music for the Baptist, but the Baptist wouldn't dance. They threw a party for the Baptist, but the Baptist wouldn't come. The Baptist's friends find it awfully difficult to know how to take him.

And yet, by all accounts, the Baptist seems to be such an important personage. By all accounts, though rarely visible, the Baptist seems to make his unseen influence felt by everybody about the place. I wonder why that is so?

The Son of Man is an awfully sociable fellow. The Son of Man loves society. The Son of Man loves invitations. The Son of Man loves dinners. The Son of Man loves all that sort of thing. The Son of Man is an awfully sociable fellow.

The Son of Man's friends find it awfully difficult to know how to take him. They played funeral songs for the Son of Man, but the Son of Man wouldn't cry. They held a fast for the Son of Man, but the Son of Man wouldn't give up food and drink. The Son of Man's friends find it awfully difficult to know how to take him.

And yet, by all accounts, the Son of Man seems to be such an important personage. By all accounts, though rarely visible, the Son of Man seems to make his unseen influence felt by everybody about the place. I wonder why that is so?

Pray that our eyes may be open, then, and that we may be willing to recognise the presence of the eternal God, both in the feast *and* in the fast, both in the wedding dance *and* in the funeral lament.

PRAYER
Lord God,
you set before your people
the fasting of the Baptist
and the feasting of the Son of Man.
Help us to recognise your presence
in the wedding feast and in the dance,
in the funeral song and in the lament;
for your presence makes holy
the whole of life,
now and for ever.

Amen

# Episode 12:
# Listening to nature

*Jesus said, 'Look how the wild flowers grow.'*

THE WILD WOOD

Mole was sitting by the winter fire side. Such a rich time it had been, when one came to look back on it all! ... The pageant of the river bank had marched steadily along, unfolding itself in scene-pictures that succeeded each other in stately procession. Purple loosestrife arrived early, shaking luxuriant tangled locks along the edge of the mirror whence its own face laughed back at it. Willow-herb, tender and wistful, like a pink sunset cloud was not slow to follow. Comfrey, the purple hand-in-hand with the white, crept forth to take its place in the line; and at last one morning the diffident and delaying dog-rose stepped delicately on the stage, and one knew, as if string music had announced it in stately chords that strayed into a gavotte, that June at last was here. One member of the company was still awaited; the shepherd-boy for the nymphs to woo, the knight for whom the ladies waited at the window, the prince that was to kiss the sleeping summer back to life and love. But when meadow-sweet, debonair and odorous in amber jerkin, moved graciously to his place in the group, then the play was ready to begin.

MATTHEW 6:28 – 33

Jesus continued, 'And why worry about clothes? Look how the wild flowers grow: they do not work or make clothes for themselves. But I tell you that not even King Solomon with all his wealth had clothes as beautiful as one of these flowers. It is God who clothes the wild grass – grass that is here today and gone tomorrow, burnt up in the oven. Won't he be all the more sure to clothe you? How little faith you have!

'So do not start worrying: "Where will my food come from? or my drink? or my clothes?" (These are the things the pagans are always concerned about.) Your Father in heaven knows that you need all these things. Instead, be concerned above everything else with the Kingdom of God and with what he requires of you, and he will provide you with all these other things.'

MEDITATION

The Mole was such an observant fellow. The whole of the river bank caught and kept his attention. With eyes to see, the Mole saw the purple loosestrife and the pink willow herb. With ears to hear, the Mole heard the rustle of the leaves and the gentle splashing of the river. With paws to feel, the Mole felt the warming of the sun and the chilling of the breeze. With nose to smell, the Mole sniffed the odorous meadow-sweet and the delicate dog-rose. With mouth to taste, the Mole savoured the first fruits of the summer and the ripened fruits of autumn. The Mole was such an observant fellow.

The Mole was such a perceptive fellow. The whole of

the river bank pointed beyond itself to its own deeper significance. With eyes to see to the heart of the matter, the Mole knew precisely when the play was ready to begin. The Mole was such a perceptive fellow.

The Galilean preacher was such an observant fellow. The whole of the created order caught and kept his attention. With eyes to see, the Galilean preacher saw the wild flowers of the field and the grasses growing in the desert. With ears to hear, the Galilean preacher heard the birds in the branches of the mustard tree and the breeze whistle through the bare branches that bore no figs. With hands to feel, the Galilean preacher felt the sun that ripened the grain and the moisture that nurtured the seed. With nose to smell, the Galilean preacher sniffed the fragrance of the lilies of the field and the earthiness of the newly dug soil. With mouth to taste, the Galilean preacher savoured the fruits of the vine and the ripened grain of the Sabbath-protected field. The Galilean preacher was such an observant fellow.

The Galilean preacher was such a perceptive fellow. The whole of the created order pointed beyond itself to the deeper significance of the Kingdom of God among us. With eyes to see to the heart of the matter, the Galilean preacher saw through the colourful clothes of the wild flowers to God's eternal commitment to clothe the people of God. With ears to hear to the heart of the matter, the Galilean preacher heard through the well-fed song of the birds of the air to God's eternal concern to nourish the people of God. With hands to feel to the heart of the matter, the Galilean preacher felt through the nurturing rain and the ripening sun to God's eternal work in nurturing the souls of men and women. The Galilean preacher was such a perceptive fellow.

Pray, then, that we may share such powers of observation into the world around us and such powers of perception into the Kingdom of God among us.

PRAYER
Lord Jesus Christ,
you saw through the flowers of the field
into the very heart of the Kingdom of God.
Open our eyes to the world around us
and open our minds to the Kingdom among us;
for you are our God,
now and always.

Amen.

# Episode 13: Breaking Free

*Scripture says that the younger son left home and went to a country far away.*

## THE WILD WOOD

There was plenty to talk about on those short winter days when the animals found themselves round the fire; still, the Mole had a good deal of spare time on his hands, and so one afternoon, when the Rat in his arm-chair before the blaze was alternately dozing and trying over rhymes that wouldn't fit, he formed the resolution to go out by himself and explore the Wild Wood, and perhaps strike up an acquaintance with Mr Badger.

It was a cold still afternoon with a hard steely sky overhead, when he slipped out of the warm parlour into the open air. The country lay bare and entirely leafless around him, and he thought that he had never seen so far and so intimately into the insides of things as on that winter day when Nature was deep in her annual slumber and seemed to have kicked the clothes off. Copses, dells, quarries and all hidden places, which had been mysterious mines for exploration in leafy summer, now exposed themselves and their secrets pathetically, and seemed to ask him to overlook their shabby poverty for a while, till they could riot in rich masquerade as before, and trick and entice him with the old deceptions. It was pitiful in a way, and yet cheering – even exhilarating. He was glad that he liked the country undecorated, hard, and stripped of its finery. ... With great cheerfulness of spirit he pushed on towards the Wild Wood, which lay before him low and threatening, like a back reef in some still southern sea.

## LUKE 15:11 – 13

Jesus went on to say, 'There was once a man who had two sons. The younger one said to him, "Father, give me my share of the property now." So the man divided his property between his two sons. After a few days the younger son sold his part of the property and left home with the money. He went to a country far away, where he wasted his money in reckless living.'

## MEDITATION

It was all quite innocent really. Certainly the Mole was not a bad creature. Certainly the Mole was not a rebellious creature. The Mole just wanted to go exploring. It was all quite innocent really.

Life with the Rat down by the riverbank was all too predictable. With short winter days and long winter nights, the Mole had a good deal of spare time on his hands. The Rat just sat in his armchair before the blazing fire, alternately dozing and trying over rhymes that wouldn't fit. Life with the Rat down by the riverbank was all too predictable.

It was all quite understandable really. The Mole just wanted to find out what life was really like in the Wild Wood. The Mole just wanted to experience for himself that ultimate encounter with the Badger. It was all quite understandable really.

But at the time it felt all rather different to the Rat. The Rat, you see, had been in the Wild Wood. The Rat, you see, had met the Badger. The Rat, you see, knew the danger. It felt all rather different to the Rat.

But how else could the Mole have learnt for himself the lessons of life?

It was all quite innocent really. Certainly the younger son was not a bad creature. Certainly the younger son was not a rebellious creature. The younger son just wanted to go exploring. It was all quite innocent really.

Life with his father down on the farm was all too predictable. With short winter days and long winter nights, the younger son had a great deal of spare time on his hands. The father just sat in his armchair before the blazing fire, alternately dozing and trying over recipes for the fatted calf. Life with the father down on the farm was all too predictable.

It was all quite understandable really. The younger son just wanted to find out what life was really like in the wild world. The younger son just wanted to experience for himself that ultimate encounter with the people who really matter. It was all quite understandable really.

But at the time it felt all rather different to the father. The father, you see, had been in the wild world. The father, you see, had experienced for himself the people who really matter. The father, you see, knew the danger. If felt all rather different to the father.

But how else could the younger son have learnt for himself the lessons of life?

Pray, then, that with the Rat and with the father you may have the wisdom to allow others to make their own mistakes, and the grace to forgive them the hurt they cause.

PRAYER
Lord Jesus Christ,
you never condemned people
for making their own mistakes.
Help us to respect the freedom of others
and to forgive the hurt their freedom causes to us.
We make our prayer in your name.

Amen.

# Episode 14:
# Cloak of darkness

*Jesus said, 'People love darkness rather than light.'*

THE WILD WOOD

There was nothing to alarm the Mole at first entry. Twigs crackled under his feet, logs tripped him, funguses on stumps resembled caricatures, and startled him for the moment by their likeness to something familiar and far away; but that was all fun, and exciting. It led him on, and he penetrated to where the light was less, and trees crouched nearer and nearer, and holes made ugly mouths at him on either side.

Everything was very still now. The dusk advanced on him steadily, rapidly, gathering in behind and before; and the light seemed to be draining away like flood-water.

Then the faces began.

It was over his shoulder, and indistinctly, that he first thought he saw a face: a little evil wedge-shaped face, looking out at him from a hole. When he turned and confronted it, the thing had vanished.

He quickened his pace, telling himself cheerfully not to begin imagining things, or there would be simply no end to it. He passed another hole, and another, and another; and then ... suddenly, and as if it had been so all the time, every hole, far and near, and there were hundreds of them, seemed to possess its face, coming and going rapidly, all fixing on him glances of malice and hatred: all hard-eyed and evil and sharp.

## JOHN 3:19 – 21

Jesus said, 'This is how the judgement works: the light has come into the world, but people love the darkness rather than the light, because their deeds are evil. Anyone who does evil things hates the light and will not come to the light, because he does not want his evil deeds to be shown up. But whoever does what is true comes to the light in order that the light may show that what he did was in obedience to God.'

## MEDITATION

It was dark, dark, dark in the Wild Wood. The last fading rays of the glimmering sun had long since fled to safety. Dusk had turned to blackness. The shades and shadows of night had closed rank. Light had drained away like flood-water. It was dark, dark, dark in the Wild Wood.

Under the cloak of darkness, the true character of the Wild Wood shone bright. Little evil wedge-shaped faces emerged from black gaping holes. Glances of malice and hatred, all hard-eyed and evil and sharp, danced across the blackness of the night. Under the cloak of darkness, the true character of the Wild Wood shone bright.

It was dark, dark, dark when Judas Iscariot went out into the night. The last fading rays of the glimmering sun had long since fled to safety. Dusk had turned to blackness. The shades and shadows of night had closed rank. Light had drained away like flood-water. It was dark, dark, dark when Judas Iscariot went out into the night.

Under the cloak of darkness, the true character of Judas Iscariot shone bright. Little evil wedge-shaped ideas emerged from the black gaping soul. Glances of malice and hatred, all hard-eyed and evil and sharp, danced across the blackness of the night. Under the cloak of darkness, the true character of Judas Iscariot shone bright.

It was dark, dark, dark when the crowd armed with swords and clubs came into the garden of Gethsemane. The last fading rays of the glimmering sun had long since fled to safety. Dusk had turned to blackness. The shades and shadows of night had closed rank. Light had drained away like flood-water. It was dark, dark, dark when the crowd armed with swords and clubs came into the garden of Gethsemane.

Under the cloak of darkness, the true character of the bloodthirsty crowd shone bright. Little evil wedge-shaped faces emerged from black gaping holes. Glances of malice and hatred, all hard-eyed and evil and sharp, danced across the blackness of the night. Under the cloak of darkness, the true character of the bloodthirsty crowd shone bright.

It was dark, dark, dark when the Son of God cried with a loud voice, 'Eloi, Eloi, lema Sabachthani?' and breathed his last. The last blistering rays of the midday sun had long since fled to safety. Noontide had rushed to blackness. The shades and shadows of night had captured the territory of the day. Light had been banished from the sky. It was dark, dark, dark when the Son of God cried with a loud voice, 'Eloi, Eloi, lema Sabachthani?' and breathed his last.

Under the cloak of darkness, the true character of the Son of God shone bright. Outstretched arms embraced a fallen world. A saviour's blood washed white the sin-stained soul. A dying voice pronounced forgiveness on those who stole his breath. Under the cloak of darkness, the character of the Son of God shone bright.

PRAYER
Lord Jesus Christ,
you are the true light,
that no darkness ever quenches.
Illuminate the recesses of our lives,
that we may turn away
from all the deeds of darkness.
We make our prayer in your name.

Amen.

# Episode 15: Seeking the lost

*Jesus said, 'Your father in heaven does not
want any of these little ones to be lost.'*

THE WILD WOOD

The Rat left the house and carefully examined the muddy
surface of the ground outside, hoping to find the Mole's
tracks. There they were, sure enough. The goloshes were
new, just bought for the winter, and the pimples on their
soles were fresh and sharp. He could see the imprints of
them in the mud, running along straight and purposeful,
leading direct to the Wild Wood.

The Rat looked very grave, and stood in deep thought
for a minute or two. Then he re-entered the house,
strapped a belt round his waist, shoved a brace of pistols
into it, took up a stout cudgel that stood in a corner of the
hall, and set off for the Wild Wood at a smart pace.

It was already getting towards dusk when he reached
the first fringe of trees and plunged without hesitation
into the wood, looking anxiously on either side for any
sign of his friend. Here and there wicked little faces
popped out of holes, but vanished immediately at sight of
the valorous animal, his pistols, and the great ugly cudgel
in his grasp; and the whistling and pattering, which he
had heard quite plainly on his first entry, died away and
ceased, and all was very still. He made his way manfully

through the length of the wood, to its furthest edge; then, forsaking all paths, he set himself to traverse it, laboriously working over the whole ground, and all the time calling out cheerfully, 'Moly, Moly, Moly! Where are you? It's me – it's old Rat!'

## MATTHEW 18:12 – 14

Jesus continued, 'What do you think a man does who has a hundred sheep and one of them gets lost? He will leave the other ninety-nine grazing on the hillside and go and look for the lost sheep. When he finds it, I tell you, he feels far happier over this one sheep than over the ninety-nine that did not get lost. In just the same way your Father in heaven does not want any of these little ones to be lost.'

## MEDITATION

There are no two ways about it. The Rat was a foolish fellow. The night was dark. The weather was bad. The Wild Wood was dangerous. The cause was a hopeless one from the very start. The Rat was a foolish fellow.

There are no two ways about it. The Rat was under no obligation to follow. He had advised the Mole. He had warned the Mole. He had forbidden the Mole. He had done all that could be done. The Rat was under no obligation to follow.

There are no two ways about it. The Rat should have stopped to count the cost. He was risking limb and life. What use is a brace of pistols in the face of all the hostile forces of the wild Wild Wood? He was risking life and limb. What help is a stout cudgel against the evil forces of the night? The Rat should have stopped to count the cost.

There are no two ways about it. The Rat should have

left the Mole to find his own way home. The Mole was brave enough to make his own decisions. The Mole was brave enough to accept responsibility for himself. After all, the Mole had left footprints in the mud and could, therefore, retrace his steps. The Rat should have left the Mole to find his own way home.

There are no two ways about it. The good shepherd was a foolish fellow. The night was dark. The weather was bad. The countryside was dangerous. The cause was a hopeless one from the very start. The good shepherd was a foolish fellow.

There are no two ways about it. The good shepherd was under no obligation to follow. He had advised the sheep. He had warned the sheep. He had forbidden the sheep. He had done all that could be done. The good shepherd was under no obligation to follow.

There are no two ways about it. The good shepherd should have stopped to count the cost. He was risking limb and life. What use is a brace of gospels in the face of all the hostile forces of the wild wild world? He was risking life and limb. What help is a stout pastoral crook against the evil forces of the night? The good shepherd should have stopped to count the cost.

There are no two ways about it. The good shepherd should have left the errant sheep to find his own way home. The errant sheep was brave enough to make his own decisions. The errant sheep was brave enough to accept responsibility for himself. The good shepherd should have left the errant sheep to find his own way home. After all, what performance indicator could demand more than 99% success?

Give thanks that the good shepherd *is* such a foolish fellow. Give thanks that the good shepherd seeks you when you are lost. And pray that you may follow in such footsteps of foolishness.

PRAYER
Lord Jesus Christ,
you are the good shepherd.
You came to seek the lost
and lost your life in the seeking.
Send us out in your name
to proclaim the good news to the lost
and salvation to the fallen,
through the power of your resurrection life.

Amen.

## CHAPTER FOUR

# *Coming face to face with face with Mr Badger*

# Episode 16:
# Waiting patiently

*Scripture says, 'Simeon was a good, devout man and was waiting for Israel to be saved.'*

MR BADGER

They waited patiently for what seemed a very long time, stamping in the snow to keep their feet warm. At last they heard the sound of slow shuffling footsteps approaching the door from the inside. It seemed, as the Mole remarked to the Rat, like some one walking in carpet slippers that were too large for him and down at heel; which was intelligent of Mole, because that was exactly what it was.

There was the noise of a bolt shot back, and the door opened a few inches, enough to show a long snout and a pair of sleepy blinking eyes.

'Now, the *very* next time this happens,' said a gruff and suspicious voice, 'I shall be exceedingly angry. Who is it *this* time, disturbing people on such a night? Speak up!'

'O, Badger,' cried the Rat, 'let us in, please. It's me, Rat, and my friend Mole, and we've lost our way in the snow.'

'What, Ratty, my dear little man!' exclaimed the Badger, in quite a different voice. 'Come along in, both of you, at once. Why, you must be perished. Well I never! Lost in the snow! And in the Wild Wood too, and at this time of night! But come in with you.'

## LUKE 2:25 – 32

At that time there was a man named Simeon living in Jerusalem. He was a good, devout man and was waiting for Israel to be saved. The Holy Spirit was with him and had assured him that he would not die before he had seen the Lord's promised Messiah. Led by the Spirit, Simeon went into the Temple. When the parents brought the child Jesus into the Temple to do for him what the Law required, Simeon took the child in his arms and gave thanks to God:

'Now, Lord, you have kept your promise,
and you may let your servant go in peace.
With my own eyes I have seen your salvation, which
you have prepared in the presence of all peoples:
A light to reveal your will to the Gentiles.'

## MEDITATION

The Mole had waited, waited for a long long time. He had waited through the long long summer to come face to face with Mr Badger. But nothing, nothing had happened.

And now tonight the Mole had waited, waited for a long long time. He had waited in the cold cold snow for the door to open into the burrow and for the first glimmer of light to break through. But nothing, nothing had happened.

And now at last, in the midst of the long long wait, there was expectancy in the air. Mole's ears pricked up as he caught the distant sound of shuffling feet. Mole's eyes lit up as he glimpsed the first chink of light breaking through the door opening into the great inside. Mole's arms shot up as he stretched out to grasp the offer of salvation.

The Mole had waited, waited for a long long time. Then at long long last all the waiting, all the longing were rewarded by the life-transforming encounter. In unison with the Rat, the Mole exclaimed, 'O Badger, let us in, please. We have lost our way in the snow.'

Simeon, too, had waited, waited for a long long time. He had waited through his long long life to come face to face with the Lord's anointed one. But nothing, nothing had happened.

And now today Simeon had waited, waited for a long long time. He had waited in the cold cold temple for the door to open into God's long-promised future and for the first glimmer of the long-promised light to break through. But nothing, nothing had happened.

And now at last, in the midst of the long long wait, there was expectancy in the air. Simeon's ears pricked up as he caught the distant sound of shuffling feet. Simeon's eyes lit up as he glimpsed the first chink of light breaking through the door opening into the great beyond. Simeon's arms shot up as he stretched out to grasp the offer of the saviour.

Simeon had waited, waited for a long long time. Then at long long last all the waiting, all the longing were rewarded by the life-transforming encounter. In unison with the whole human race, Simeon exclaimed, 'O light of the nations, let us in, please. We have lost our way in the world.'

Pray, then, that we may share Mole's patient expectancy in times of cold and darkness, when the waiting and the longing appear so unrewarded. Pray, too, that we may recognise the distant shuffling of the slippers and respond to the dawning of God's promised light.

PRAYER
Lord Jesus Christ,
you opened Simeon's eyes to your light
and filled his arms with your presence.
Give us patience to await your coming
and the joy of welcoming your light in our lives;
for in you is our hope,
now and always.

Amen.

# Episode 17: Open table

*Scripture says, 'Many of them joined Jesus and his disciples at the table.'*

## MR BADGER

'But come along,' said the Badger, 'come into the kitchen. There's a first-rate fire there, and supper and everything.'

He shuffled on in front of them, carrying the light, and they followed him, nudging each other in an anticipating sort of way, down a long ... passage, into a sort of a central hall ... . But there were doors in the hall as well – stout oaken comfortable-looking doors. One of these the Badger flung open, and at once they found themselves in all the glow and warmth of a large fire-lit kitchen.

The floor was well-worn red brick, and on the wide hearth burnt a fire of logs, between two attractive chimney-corners tucked away in the wall, well out of any suspicion of draught. A couple of high-backed settles, facing each other on either side of the fire, gave further sitting accommodation for the sociably disposed. In the middle of the room stood a long table of plain boards placed on trestles, with benches down each side.... Rows of spotless plates winked from the shelves of the dresser at the far end of the room, and from the rafters overhead hung hams, bundles of dried herbs, nets of onions, and baskets of eggs. It seemed a place where heroes could fitly feast after victory, where weary harvesters could line up in scores along the table and keep their Harvest Home with mirth and song, or where two or three friends of simple tastes could sit about as they pleased and eat and smoke and talk in comfort and contentment.

## MARK 2:15 – 17

Later on Jesus was having a meal in his house. A large number of tax collectors and other outcasts was following Jesus, and many of them joined him and his disciples at the table. Some teachers of the Law, who were Pharisees, saw that Jesus was eating with these outcasts and tax collectors, so they asked his disciples, 'Why does he eat with such people?'

Jesus heard them and answered, 'People who are well do not need a doctor, but only those who are sick. I have not come to call respectable people, but outcasts.'

## MEDITATION

It seems as if the open table was always, always there at the heart of the Badger's house. The red brick floor was well worn by the stamping of many feet. The plain boards of the table, so well shaped in the carpenter's workshop, were well marked by the scraping of many hands. The rows of spotless plates winked from the shelves to welcome the many guests. It seems as if the open table was always, always there at the heart of the Badger's house.

It seems as if starving guests were always, always beating a path to the Badger's open table. Today it is the Rat and the Mole for an impromptu supper. Tomorrow it is the two young hedgehogs for an unplanned breakfast of bacon and eggs. Individually and together they stand shoulder to shoulder with the triumphant heroes (and heroines) who feast after victory, with the mirthful harvesters who celebrate after wearisome labour, and with the two or three intimate friends who eat and smoke and talk in comfort and contentment. It seems as if starving guests were always, always beating a path to the Badger's open table.

For the Mole, however, these apparent and eternal truths appear today as a stunning and startling revelation. And all Mole needed to do to unlock the secret was respond to the simple invitation to follow the Badger along the passage that leads to the kitchen.

It seems as if the open table was always, always there at the heart of Jesus' house. The simple floor was well worn by the stamping of many feet. The plain boards of the table, so well shaped by the master carpenter of Nazareth, were well marked by the scraping of many hands. The rows of spotless plates winked from the shelves to welcome the many guests. It seems as if the open table was always, always there at the heart of Jesus' house.

It seems as if starving guests were always, always beating a path to Jesus' open table. Today it is Levi, the tax collector, for an impromptu supper. Tomorrow it is Peter and Andrew for an unplanned breakfast of fish and bread. Individually and together they stand shoulder to shoulder with the triumphant teachers of the law (and Pharisees) who seek after victory, with the mirthful outcasts and tax collectors who celebrate after changing their whole lifestyle, and with the two or three intimate disciples who eat and pray and talk in comfort and contentment. It seems as if starving guests were always, always beating a path to Jesus' open table.

For Levi, however, these apparent and eternal truths appear today as a stunning and startling revelation. And all Levi needed to do to unlock the secret was to respond to the simple invitation to follow Jesus along the passage that leads to the Kingdom of God.

Give thanks, then, that Mole discovered the secret of the open table and pray that others may come to stand today, for the very first time, where Levi stood, shoulder to shoulder with the countless generations who have beaten a path to Jesus' open table.

PRAYER
Lord Jesus Christ,
your table is open
to all peoples of the world.
Help us to hear your invitation,
to accept your welcome
and to feel at home
with all your many guests;
for you are our God,
now and for ever.

Amen.

# Episode 18: Real service

*Scripture says, 'Jesus poured some water into a basin and began to wash the disciples' feet.'*

MR BADGER
The kindly Badger thrust them down on a settle to toast themselves at the fire, and bade them remove their wet coats and boots. Then he fetched them dressing-gowns and slippers, and himself bathed the Mole's shin with warm water and mended the cut with sticking-plaster till the whole thing was just as good as new, if not better. In the embracing light and warmth, warm and dry at last, with weary legs propped up in front of them, and a suggestive clink of plates being arranged on the table behind, it seemed to the storm-driven animals, now in safe anchorage, that the cold and trackless Wild Wood just left outside was miles and miles away, and all that they had suffered in it a half-forgotten dream.

JOHN 13: 4 – 9
Jesus ... rose from the table, took off his outer garment, and tied a towel round his waist. Then he poured some water into a basin and began to wash the disciples' feet and dry them with the towel round his waist. He came to Simon Peter, who said to him, 'Are you going to wash my feet, Lord?'

Jesus answered him, 'You do not understand now what I am doing, but you will understand later.'

Peter declared, 'Never at any time will you wash my feet!'

'If I do not wash your feet,' Jesus answered, 'you will no longer be my disciple.'

Simon Peter answered, 'Lord, do not wash only my feet, then! Wash my hands and head, too!'

MEDITATION

Without doubt, the Badger presided at the feast. As president, he opened the door to the subterranean burrow and invited in the guests. He led the way through the labyrinth of passages and installed the Mole and the Rat around the warmly glowing hearth. He planned the menu and provided the food at his own expense. He took the armchair at the head of the table and said the blessing before the meal began. Without doubt, the Badger presided at the feast.

Without doubt, the Badger served at the feast. As servant, he stoked the fire and swept clean the hearth. He scrubbed the table and set out the plates. He prepared the food and arranged it in the dishes. Without doubt, the Badger served at the feast.

Without doubt, the Badger waited on the guests. Before the meal began, he bade them remove their wet coats and boots. He fetched them dressing-gowns and slippers. He tied a towel round his waist and poured water into a basin. He bathed the Mole's wounded shin and mended the cut with sticking plaster until the whole leg was just as good as new, if not better. Without doubt, the Badger waited on the guests.

Without doubt, Jesus, too, presided at the feast. As

president, he opened the door to the upper room and invited in the guests. He led the way through the labyrinth of the Passover ritual and installed the disciples around the Paschal table. He planned the hiring of the room and provided the food at his own expense. He took the armchair at the head of the table and said the blessing over the bread and over the wine. Without doubt, Jesus presided at the feast.

Without doubt, Jesus served at the feast. As servant, he scrubbed the table and set out the plates. He prepared the symbolic food of the Passover meal and arranged the bitter herbs in the dishes. Without doubt, Jesus served at the feast.

Without doubt, Jesus waited on the guests. He rose from the table and bade them remove their dirty coats and boots. He took off his own outer garment, and tied a towel round his waist and poured water into a basin. He bathed Simon Peter's feet and mended his wounded soul with sticking plaster until the whole person was just as good as new, if not better. Without doubt, Jesus waited on the guests.

Pray, then, that like Mole, like Peter, you may experience both the presidency and the service of the master of the feast.


PRAYER
Lord Jesus Christ,
you are president at the feast
and servant to your guests.
Give us grace to acknowledge your presidency
and humility to accept your service.
We make our prayer in your name.

Amen.

# Episode 19:
# Finding acceptance

*Jesus said, 'I do not condemn you either.'*

MR BADGER

Conversation was impossible for a long time; and when it was slowly resumed, it was that regrettable sort of conversation that results from talking with your mouth full. The Badger did not mind that sort of thing at all, nor did he take any notice of elbows on the table, or everybody speaking at once. ... He sat in his arm-chair at the head of the table, and nodded gravely at intervals as the animals told their story; and he did not seem surprised or shocked at anything, and he never said, 'I told you so,' or, 'Just what I always said,' or remarked that they ought to have done so-and-so, or ought not to have done something else. The Mole began to feel very friendly towards him.

When supper was really finished at last, and each animal felt that his skin was now as tight as was decently safe, and that by this time he didn't care a hang for anybody or anything, they gathered round the glowing embers of the great wood fire, and thought how jolly it was to be sitting up *so* late, and *so* independent, and *so* full; and after they had chatted for a long time about things in general, the Badger said heartily, 'Now then! tell us the news from your part of the world. How's old Toad going on?'

JOHN 8:3 – 11
The teachers of the Law and the Pharisees brought in a woman who had been caught committing adultery, and they made her stand before them all. 'Teacher,' they said to Jesus, 'this woman was caught in the very act of committing adultery. In our Law Moses commanded that such a woman must be stoned to death. Now, what do you say?' They said this to trap Jesus, so that they could accuse him. But he bent over and wrote on the ground with his finger.

As they stood there asking him questions, he straightened himself up and said to them, 'Whichever one of you has committed no sin may throw the first stone at her.' Then he bent over again and wrote on the ground. When they heard this, they all left, one by one, the older ones first. Jesus was left alone, with the woman still standing there. He straightened himself up and said to her, 'Where are they? Is there no one left to condemn you?'

'No one, sir,' she answered.

'Well, then,' Jesus said, 'I do not condemn you either. Go, but do not sin again.'

MEDITATION
It would have been so easy for the Badger to have condemned. The Rat and the Mole arrived at the most inconvenient of times. The Badger had already dressed for bed, found his favourite slippers and lit the night-time candle. It would have been so easy for the Badger to have said, 'Get lost; go away!'

It would have been so easy for the Badger to have condemned. The Rat and the Mole made little attempt to be gracious guests. Theirs was that regrettable sort of conversation which results from talking with your mouth full. It would have been so easy for the Badger to have said, 'You ought to mind your manners!'

It would have been so easy for the Badger to have condemned. The Rat and the Mole told him tales of their behaviour in the wild Wild Wood, and bared the deepest secrets of their innermost souls. It would have been so easy for the Badger to have seemed surprised or shocked, and to have exclaimed, 'I told you so!'

It would have been so easy for the Badger to have condemned. Instead, he nodded gravely at intervals as the animals told their tale. Then he sent them away, acquitted and freed, forgiven and rehabilitated. It was easy for the Badger to accept.

It would have been so easy for Jesus, also, to have condemned. The teachers of the Law and the Pharisees arrived at the most inconvenient of times. Jesus had already planned his lessons for the day and found his favourite text. It would have been so easy for Jesus to have said, 'Get lost; go away!'

It would have been so easy for Jesus to have condemned. The teachers of the Law and the Pharisees made little attempt to be gracious guests. Theirs was that regrettable sort of conversation that tries to trick and to trap, to catch and to deceive. It would have been so easy for Jesus to have said, 'You ought to mind your manners!'

It would have been so easy for Jesus to have condemned. The teachers of the Law and the Pharisees told him tales of the woman's behaviour in the wild wild world, and bared the deepest secrets of her innermost soul. It would have been so easy for Jesus to have seemed surprised or shocked, and to have exclaimed, 'I told you so!'

It would have been so easy for Jesus to have condemned. Instead, he bent over and wrote on the ground with his finger, as the teachers of the Law and the Pharisees told their tale. Then he sent the woman away, acquitted and freed, forgiven and rehabilitated. It was easy for Jesus to accept.

Give thanks, then, that Mole and Rat experienced such acceptance in the Badger's presence; and that the woman experienced such acceptance in Jesus' presence. Pray, too, that we may experience the acceptance that Jesus offers us, and extend that acceptance to others in our daily lives.

PRAYER
Lord Jesus Christ,
you accept us as we are
and renew us by your acceptance.
Help us to accept others in your name
and to extend to all your acceptance and love;
for you are our Lord,
now and always.

Amen.

# Episode 20: Keeping busy

*Jesus said, 'Let us go off by ourselves to
some place where we will be alone
and you can rest for a while.'*

## MR BADGER

'Where's Mr Badger?' inquired the Mole, as he warmed the coffee-pot before the fire.

'The master's gone into his study, sir,' replied the hedgehog, 'and he said as how he was going to be particular busy this morning, and on no account was he to be disturbed.'

This explanation, of course, was thoroughly understood by every one present. The fact is, as already set forth, when you live a life of intense activity for six months in the year, and of comparative or actual somnolence for the other six, during the latter period you cannot be continually pleading sleepiness when there are people about or things to be done. The excuse gets monotonous. The animals well knew that Badger, having eaten a hearty breakfast, had retired to his study and settled himself in an arm-chair with his legs up on another and a red cotton handkerchief over his face, and was being 'busy' in the usual way at this time of the year.

MARK 6:30 – 32

The apostles returned and met with Jesus, and told him all they had done and taught. There were so many people coming and going that Jesus and his disciples didn't even have time to eat. So he said to them, 'Let us go off by ourselves to some place where we will be alone and you can rest for a while.' So they started out in a boat by themselves for a lonely place.

MEDITATION

The Badger knows that there are many ways of keeping busy. Yesterday he was busy in the outer world of people, relationships with others, and public affairs. Yesterday he welcomed strangers who pounded on his door. Yesterday he warmed the dispirited Rat, repaired the wounded Mole, fed the hungry visitors, reclothed the naked travellers, washed the grubby guests, and engaged in endless conversation.

The Badger knows that there are many ways of keeping busy. Today he is busy in the inner world of ideas, relationships with the inner self and personal affairs. Today he closes the study door. Today he warms the chilled soul, feeds the hungry spirit, reclothes the intellect, washes the grubby mind, repairs the wounded feelings, and explores the inner depths.

The Badger knows that there are many ways of keeping busy, and he has wisely taught his friends to distinguish between them, and to respect the different modes of busyness.

Jesus, too, knows that there are many ways of keeping busy. Yesterday he was busy in the outer world of people, relationships with others, and public affairs. Yesterday he welcomed strangers who pounded on his door or who removed the roof to let in their paralysed friend. Yesterday he had lit a fire by the lakeside to warm the dispirited fishermen. Yesterday he had spotted five thousand hungry people clustering around five loaves and two small fishes. Yesterday he had reclothed the demoniac in his rightful mind. Yesterday he had washed the grubby feet of travel-weary disciples. Yesterday he had bound up the broken-hearted and repaired the sin-stained soul. Yesterday he had engaged in endless dialogue about the Kingdom of God and the ways of blessedness.

Jesus knows that there are many ways of keeping busy. Today he is busy in the inner world of ideas, relationships with the inner self and personal affairs. Today he closes the study door. Today he warms the chilled soul, feeds the hungry spirit, reclothes the bare intellect, refreshes the weary mind, repairs the wounded feelings, and explores the inner depths and strengthens the life of prayer.

Jesus knows that there are many ways of keeping busy, and he has wisely taught his disciples to follow his example, to distinguish between them and to respect the different modes of busyness.

Give thanks, then, that Mr Badger had the wisdom to know that there are many ways of keeping busy. And pray that, in your service for the Kingdom of God, you may have the wisdom to keep yourselves properly busy, both in the outer world of relationships and public affairs and in the inner world of your own spiritual depths.

PRAYER
Lord Jesus Christ,
you taught your disciples
to give themselves to the service of others
and to make space for themselves.
Give us wisdom
to serve you without reservation
and to keep ourselves fit for your service;
for your name's sake.

Amen.

## CHAPTER FIVE
# *Dulce Domum*

# Episode 21: Looking back

*Scripture says, 'Peter took Jesus aside
and began to rebuke him.'*

DULCE DOMUM

The Rat was walking a little way ahead, as his habit was,
his shoulders humped, his eyes fixed on the straight grey
road in front of him; so he did not notice poor Mole when
suddenly the summons reached him, and took him like
an electric shock....

The call was clear, the summons was plain. He must
obey it instantly, and go. 'Ratty!' he called, full of joyful
excitement, 'hold on! Come back! I want you, quick!'

'O, *come* along, Mole, do!' replied the Rat cheerfully,
still plodding along.

'*Please* stop, Ratty!' pleaded the poor Mole, in anguish
of heart. 'You don't understand! It's my home, my old
home! I've just come across the smell of it, and it's close
by here, really quite close. And I *must* go to it, I must, I
must! O, come back, Ratty! Please, please come back!'

The Rat was by this time very far ahead, too far to hear
clearly what the Mole was calling, too far to catch the sharp
note of painful appeal in his voice. And he was much taken
up with the weather, for he too could smell something –
something suspiciously like approaching snow.

'Mole, we mustn't stop now, really!' he called back.

MATTHEW 16:21 – 23

From that time on Jesus began to say plainly to his disciples, 'I must go to Jerusalem and suffer much from the elders, the chief priests, and the teachers of the Law. I will be put to death, but three days later I will be raised to life.'

Peter took him aside and began to rebuke him. 'God forbid it, Lord!' he said. 'That must never happen to you!'

Jesus turned around and said to Peter, 'Get away from me, Satan! You are an obstacle in my way, because these thoughts of yours don't come from God, but from man.'

MEDITATION

The Rat was a natural leader. It is characteristic for the natural leader to be out there in front, a little way ahead. As his habit was, he led the way, his shoulders humped, his eyes fixed on the straight grey road in front of him. The Rat was a natural leader.

The Rat expected his disciples to follow his lead. Surely, the Mole had followed in his footsteps long enough to know the score and to understand the price. 'Mole, we mustn't stop now, really!' the Rat called back. The Rat expected his disciples to follow his lead.

The Mole was not a bad disciple. He had travelled a long way since he first responded to the Rat's kindly invitation. He had left behind him his family and friends. He had shut down his house and abandoned his home.

The Mole was not a bad disciple. He had become quite a different animal since he first responded to the Rat's kindly invitation. He had adopted a new way of life. He had shaped a new set of values. He had begun to mould himself on the model of his leader.

The Mole was not a bad disciple, but he still had a

long way to go. It is only natural that images from the past should continue to haunt his memory. It is only natural that odours from the past should tease his nostrils. It is only natural that sounds from the past should reactivate old patterns of behaviour. '*Please* stop, Ratty!' pleaded the poor Mole, in anguish of heart. 'You don't understand! I've just come across the smell of it. And I *must* go to it, I must, I must. O, come back, Ratty! Please, please come back!' The Mole was not a bad disciple, but he still had a long way to go.

Jesus, too, was a natural leader. It is characteristic for the natural leader to be out there in front, a little way ahead, a little way ahead, a little way ahead of the others' understanding. As his habit was, he led the way, his shoulders humped, his eyes fixed on the straight grey road in front of him, which led relentlessly to Calvary. Jesus was a natural leader.

Jesus expected his disciples to follow his lead. Surely, Peter had followed in his footsteps long enough to know the score and to understand the price. 'Peter, we mustn't stop now, really!' Jesus called back. 'I must go to Jerusalem and suffer much from the elders, the chief priests, and the teachers of the Law. I will be put to death.' Jesus expected his disciples to follow his lead.

Peter was not a bad disciple. He had travelled a long way since he first responded to Jesus' kindly invitation. He had left behind him his family and friends. He had shut down his house and abandoned his home.

Peter was not a bad disciple. He had become quite a different person since he first responded to Jesus' kindly invitation. He had adopted a new way of life. He had shaped a new set of values. He had begun to mould himself on the model of his leader.

Peter was not a bad disciple, but he still had a long

way to go. It is only natural that images from the past should continue to haunt his memory. It is only natural that he should still sniff in his nostrils the theology of the triumphant warrior Messiah and resist the less palatable theology of the suffering servant. '*Please* stop, Jesus!' pleaded poor Peter, in anguish of heart. 'This must never happen to you!' Peter was not a bad disciple, but he still had a long way to go.

Like the Mole and like Peter, you and I still have a long way to travel on our journey of discipleship. Pray that we may stay the course.

PRAYER
Lord Jesus Christ,
you call your disciples
to follow you along unknown paths.
Help us when we fail
to understand where you are leading;
and forgive us when we long
to look back to our old ways.
We make our prayer in the name of Jesus.

Amen.

# Episode 22: Divided loyalties

*Jesus said, 'I tell you, one of you will betray me.'*

DULCE DOMUM

Poor Mole stood alone in the road, his heart torn asunder, and a big sob gathering, gathering, somewhere low down inside him, to leap up to the surface presently, he knew, in passionate escape. But even under such a test as this his loyalty to his friend stood firm. Never for a moment did he dream of abandoning him. Meanwhile, the wafts from his old home pleaded, whispered, conjured, and finally claimed him imperiously. He dared not tarry longer within their magic circle. With a wrench that tore his very heart-strings he set his face down the road and followed submissively in the track of the Rat, while faint, thin little smells, still dogging his retreating nose, reproached him for his new friendship and his callous forgetfulness.

With an effort he caught up the unsuspecting Rat, who began chattering cheerfully about what they would do when they got back, and how jolly a fire of logs in the parlour would be, and what a supper he meant to eat; never noticing his companion's silence and distressful state of mind.

MATTHEW 26:20 – 25

When it was evening, Jesus and the twelve disciples sat down to eat. During the meal Jesus said, 'I tell you, one of you will betray me.'

The disciples were very upset and began to ask him, one after the other, 'Surely, Lord, you don't mean me?'

Jesus answered, 'One who dips his bread in the dish with me will betray me. The Son of Man will die as the Scriptures say he will, but how terrible for that man who betrays the Son of Man! It would have been better for that man if he had never been born!'

Judas, the traitor, spoke up. 'Surely, Teacher, you don't mean me?' he asked.

Jesus answered, 'So you say.'


MEDITATION

Loyalty is no easy matter.

The Mole, you see, was being disloyal to his past. His past was grounded in a subterranean way of life. His past was rooted in his family and friends. His past was shaped by his own little home, his own front door and his own kitchen table.

The Mole, you see, was being disloyal to his past. He had forsaken his subterranean way of life to join Ratty on the riverbank. He had deserted his family and friends to foster new friendships among those who travelled with Ratty. He had abandoned his own little house, his own front door and his own kitchen table in favour of a new way of life.

But, then, the time came when the Mole's past once again began to catch up with him. He found himself within that magic circle in which wafts from his old home pleaded, whispered, conjured, and finally claimed him imperiously.

Loyalty is no easy matter.

The Mole, you see, was determined to persist in the disloyalty to his past. He knew that he dare not tarry longer within that magic circle. With a wrench that tore his very heart-strings, he set his face down the road and followed submissively in the track of the Rat.

Loyalty is no easy matter.

Judas, you see, was being disloyal to his past. His past was grounded in the Jewish tradition. His past was rooted in Jewish family and friends. His past was shaped by his own treasured theories of when the Messiah would come and how the Messiah would act.

Judas, you see, was being disloyal to his past. He had forsaken the Jewish tradition, as he had understood it, to join Jesus on the lakeside. He had deserted his family and friends to foster new friendships among those who travelled with Jesus. He had abandoned his own treasured theories of when the Messiah would come and how the Messiah would act, in favour of the way of life that Jesus represented.

But, then, the time came when Judas' past once again began to catch up with him. He found himself within that magic circle in which wafts from his old home pleaded, whispered, conjured, and finally claimed him imperiously.

Loyalty is no easy matter.

Judas, you see, was determined not to persist in the disloyalty to his past. He knew that he had to tarry longer within that magic circle. With a wrench that tore at the very heart of the band of disciples, Judas set his face down the road of betrayal and stalked fearlessly in the track of the Son of God.

Like the Mole and like Judas, when we choose to follow Jesus, you and I set out on a path of disloyalty to our past. Pray that we may be given grace to remain loyal to that disloyalty.

PRAYER
Lord Jesus Christ,
you call your followers
to leave their past behind
and to remain loyal to your calling.
Stand beside us when the past calls us
and keep us faithful to you.
For you are our God,
now and always.

Amen.

# Episode 23:
# Supressed emotion

*Scripture says, 'Peter went out and wept bitterly.'*

DULCE DOMUM

At last, however, when they had gone some considerable way further, and were passing some tree-stumps at the edge of a copse that bordered the road, the Rat stopped and said kindly, 'Look here, Mole, old chap, you seem dead tired. No talk left in you, and your feet dragging like lead. We'll sit down here for a minute and rest. The snow has held off so far, and the best part of our journey is over.'

The Mole subsided forlornly on a tree-stump and tried to control himself, for he felt it surely coming. The sob he had fought with so long refused to be beaten. Up and up, it forced its way to the air, and then another, and another, and others thick and fast; till poor Mole at last gave up the struggle, and cried freely and helplessly and openly, now that he knew it was all over and he had lost what he could hardly be said to have found.

The Rat, astonished and dismayed at the violence of Mole's paroxysm of grief, did not dare to speak for a while. At last he said, very quietly and sympathetically. 'What is it, old fellow? Whatever can be the matter? Tell us your trouble, and let me see what I can do.'

Poor Mole found it difficult to get any words out between the upheavals of his chest that followed one upon another so quickly and held back speech and choked it as it came.

## LUKE 22:54 – 62

They arrested Jesus and took him away into the house of the High Priest; and Peter followed at a distance. A fire had been lit in the centre of the courtyard, and Peter joined those who were sitting round it. When one of the servant-girls saw him sitting there at the fire, she looked straight at him and said, 'This man too was with Jesus!'

But Peter denied it, 'Woman, I don't even know him!'

After a little while a man noticed Peter and said, 'You are one of them, too!'

But Peter answered, 'Man, I am not!'

And about an hour later another man insisted strongly, 'There isn't any doubt that this man was with Jesus, because he also is a Galilean!'

But Peter answered, 'Man, I don't know what you are talking about!'

At once, while he was still speaking, a cock crowed. The Lord turned round and looked straight at Peter, and Peter remembered that the Lord had said to him, 'Before the cock crows tonight, you will say three times that you do not know me.' Peter went out and wept bitterly.

## MEDITATION

The Mole was doing his very very best to cope with a difficult, difficult situation. He really had no choice. He was doing his very very best to cope with a difficult, difficult situation.

For months the Mole had pinned his life on Ratty. For

months the Mole had suppressed his past. For months the Mole had treasured a bright vision for the future. He was doing his very very best to cope with a difficult, difficult situation.

But now the Mole felt left behind and deserted. Now the Mole felt that Ratty no longer understood his deepest needs. Now the Mole felt that Ratty was powerless to support his dreams and hopes. He was doing his very very best to cope with a difficult, difficult situation.

From the wellsprings of all this emotion the Mole remembered his past. The Mole recalled his basic instincts for security and for self-preservation. The Mole doubted his own direction and commitment. The Mole severely tested his loyalty to his friend and guide. He was doing his very very best to cope with a difficult, difficult situation.

Then, at last, poor Mole gave up the struggle, and cried freely and helplessly and openly, now that he knew that it was all over and he had lost what he could hardly be said to have found.

Peter, too, was doing his very very best to cope with a difficult, difficult situation. He really had no choice. He was doing his very very best to cope with a difficult, difficult situation. For months Peter had pinned his life on Jesus. For months Peter had suppressed his past. For months Peter had treasured a bright vision for the future. He was doing his very very best to cope with a difficult, difficult situation.

But now Peter felt left behind and deserted. Now Peter felt that Jesus no longer understood his deepest needs. Now Peter felt that Jesus was powerless to support his dreams and hopes. He was doing his very very best to cope with a difficult, difficult situation.

From the wellsprings of all this emotion Peter

remembered his past. Peter recalled his basic instincts for security and self-preservation. Peter doubted his own direction and commitment. Peter severely tested his loyalty to his friend and guide. He was doing his very very best to cope with a difficult, difficult situation.

Then, at last, poor Peter gave up the struggle, and cried freely and helplessly and openly, now that he knew it was all over and he had lost what he could hardly be said to have found.

There are times when you and I, like the Mole and Peter, face difficult, difficult situations, and confront crises of loyalty and faith. However we respond, pray that we may have the courage to acknowledge the underlying emotions and the self-insight to own our failures.

PRAYER
Lord Jesus Christ,
you accepted Peter's tears of loss and failure
and transformed them to tears of penitence.
Give us grace to recognise our failures
and to weep the tears of repentance;
for your own name's sake.

Amen.

# Episode 24: Real repentance

*Zacchaeus said, 'If I have cheated anyone,*
*I will pay him back four times as much.'*

DULCE DOMUM

'I called and you wouldn't listen, Rat,' said the Mole, 'and everything came back to me with a rush – and I *wanted* it! – O dear, O dear – and when you *wouldn't* turn back, Ratty – and I had to leave it, though I was smelling it all the time – I thought my heart would break. – We might have just gone and had one look at it, Ratty – only one look – it was close by – but you wouldn't turn back, Ratty, you wouldn't turn back! O dear, O dear.'

Recollection brought fresh waves of sorrow, and sobs again took full charge of him, preventing further speech.

The Rat stared straight in front of him, saying nothing, only patting Mole gently on the shoulder. After a time he muttered gloomily, 'I see it all now! What a *pig* I have been! A pig – that's me! Just a pig – a plain pig!'

He waited till Mole's sobs became gradually less stormy and more rhythmical; he waited till at last sniffs were frequent and sobs only intermittent. Then he rose from his seat, and, remarking carelessly, 'Well, now we'd better be getting on, old chap!' set off up the road again, over the toilsome way they had come.

'Wherever are you (hic) going to (hic), Ratty?' cried the tearful Mole, looking up in alarm.

'We're going to find that home of yours, old fellow,' replied the Rat pleasantly; 'so you had better come along, for it will take some finding, and we shall want your nose.'

## LUKE 19:1 – 8

Jesus went on into Jericho and was passing through. There was a chief tax collector there named Zacchaeus, who was rich. He was trying to see who Jesus was, but he was a little man and could not see Jesus because of the crowd. So he ran ahead of the crowd and climbed a sycamore tree to see Jesus, who was going to pass that way. When Jesus came to that place, he looked up and said to Zacchaeus, 'Hurry down, Zacchaeus, because I must stay in your house today.'

Zacchaeus hurried down and welcomed him with great joy. All the people who saw it started grumbling, 'This man has gone as a guest to the home of a sinner!'

Zacchaeus stood up and said to the Lord, 'Listen, sir! I will give half my belongings to the poor, and if I have cheated anyone, I will pay him back four times as much.'

## MEDITATION

Of course the Rat was not a bad animal. The Rat knew what his job was and he set out to do it well. His task was to guide the Mole through the cold night to the warmth and safety of the fireside. And he focused all his mind and all his energy to that noble end.

Of course the Rat was not a bad animal. All his physical energy was absorbed by the task in hand, and it would have been silly to pause in the cold cold night. When all was said and done, Ratty wouldn't stop.

Of course the Rat was not a bad animal. All his mental energy was absorbed by attaining his goals, and it would have been silly to open his mind to new thoughts in the cold cold night. When all was said and done, Ratty wouldn't listen.

Of course the Rat was not a bad animal. He was used to seeing the world from his own clear perspective, and it would have been silly to look at it in any other way. When all was said and done, Ratty wouldn't see things through the eyes of the Mole.

But then, suddenly, the Rat's eyes were opened and Ratty saw himself for the very first time in a different light and from a different perspective. 'I see it all now!' said the Rat. 'What a *pig* I have been! A pig – that's me! Just a pig – a plain pig!' And in that moment of revelation, the Rat turned about and faced in a new direction. So there's repentance for you. Of course the Rat was not a bad animal.

There's repentance for you.

Of course Zacchaeus was not a bad man. Zacchaeus knew what his job was and he set out to do it well. His task was to oversee the collection of taxes to sustain the proper economy. And he focused all his mind and all his energy to that noble end.

Of course Zacchaeus was not a bad man. All his physical energy was absorbed by the task in hand, and it would have been silly to act in any other way. When all was said and done, the little man wouldn't stop and take stock.

Of course Zacchaeus was not a bad man. All his mental energy was absorbed attaining his goals, and it would have been silly to open his mind to new thoughts. When all was said and done, the little man wouldn't listen to the voices of others.

Of course Zacchaeus was not a bad man. He was used to seeing the world from his own clear perspective, and it would have been silly to act in any other way. When all was said and done, the little man wouldn't see things through the eyes of the peripatetic preacher.

But, then, suddenly Zacchaeus' eyes were opened and the little man saw himself for the very first time in a different light and from a different perspective. 'I see it all now!' said Zacchaeus. 'What a *pig* I have been! A pig – that's me! Just a pig – a plain pig!' And in that moment of revelation, Zacchaeus turned about and faced in a new direction. 'Listen sir,' he said. 'I will give half my belongings to the poor, and if I have cheated anyone, I will pay him back four times as much.' So there's repentance for you. Of course Zacchaeus was not a bad man.

There's repentance for you.

Pray, then, that you and I may be helped to see ourselves from a different perspective and learn that same lesson of true repentance.


PRAYER
Lord Jesus Christ,
you call us to take stock of our lives.
Help us to see ourselves
as you see us;
and give us grace to refashion ourselves
in your image.
For you are our God,
now and always.

Amen.

# Episode 25:
# Being resourceful

*Andrew said, 'There is a boy here
who has two loaves.'*

DULCE DOMUM

The Mole struck a match, and by its light the Rat saw
that they were standing in an open space neatly swept
and sanded underfoot, and directly facing them was
Mole's little front door, with 'Mole End' painted, in
Gothic lettering, over the bell-pull at the side....

Encouraged by his inspiriting companion, the Mole
roused himself and dusted and polished with energy and
heartiness, while the Rat, running to and fro with
armfuls of fuel, soon had a cheerful blaze roaring up the
chimney. He hailed the Mole to come and warm
himself; but Mole promptly had another fit of the blues,
dropping down on a couch in dark despair and burying
his face in his duster.

'Rat,' he moaned, 'how about your supper, you poor,
cold, hungry, weary animal? I've nothing to give you –
nothing – not a crumb!'

'What a fellow you are for giving in!' said the Rat
reproachfully. 'Why, only just now I saw a sardine-opener
on the kitchen dresser, quite distinctly; and everybody

knows that means there are sardines about somewhere in the neighbourhood. Rouse yourself! Pull yourself together, and come with me and forage.'

They went and foraged accordingly, hunting through every cupboard and turned out every drawer. The result was not so very depressing after all, though of course it might have been better; a tin of sardines – a box of captain's biscuits, nearly full – and a German sausage encased in silver paper.

'There's a banquet for you!' observed the Rat, as he arranged the table. 'I know some animals who would give their ears to be sitting down to supper with us to-night.'

'No bread!' groaned the Mole dolorously; 'no butter, no –'

'No *pâté de foie gras*, no champagne!' continued the Rat, grinning.

## JOHN 6:3 – 9

Jesus went up a hill and sat down with his disciples. The time for the Passover Festival was near. Jesus looked round and saw that a large crowd was coming to him, so he asked Philip, 'Where can we buy enough food to feed all these people?' (He said this to test Philip; actually he already knew what he would do.)

Philip answered, 'For everyone to have even a little, it would take more than two hundred silver coins to buy enough bread.'

Another of his disciples, Andrew, who was Simon Peter's brother, said, 'There is a boy here who has five loaves of barley bread and two fish. But they will certainly not be enough for all these people.'

# MEDITATION

Put under pressure, the Mole all too quickly fell apart. Put under pressure, the Mole all too quickly had a fit of the blues, dropping down on a couch in dark despair and burying his face in his duster. Put under pressure, the Mole lacked all vision, the Mole lacked all hope.

Looking into the eyes of the hungry Rat, the Mole saw only the empty table. Looking into the eyes of the hungry Rat, the Mole saw only the bare cupboard. 'Rat,' he moaned, 'how about your supper, you poor, cold, hungry, weary animal? I've nothing to give you – nothing – not a crumb!' Put under pressure, the Mole lacked all vision, the Mole lacked all hope.

Put under pressure, the Rat quickly rose to the occasion. Put under pressure, the Rat quickly spotted the possibilities. Put under pressure, the Rat became an animal of vision, the Rat became an animal of hope.

Looking into the eyes of the despairing Mole, the Rat flatly refused to share his despair. 'What a fellow you are for giving in!' said the Rat reproachfully. 'What a fellow you are for giving in.'

Looking into the eyes of the despairing Mole, the Rat looked right through the despair to the very solution itself. 'Why, only just now I saw a sardine-opener on the kitchen dresser, quite distinctly; and everybody knows that means there are sardines about somewhere in the neighbourhood.' And sardines there were. The animals were fed. Put under pressure, the Rat became an animal of vision, the Rat became a prophet of hope.

Put under pressure, Philip all too quickly fell apart. Put under pressure, Philip all too quickly had a fit of the blues, dropping down on the grass in dark despair and burying his head in the sand. Put under pressure, Philip lacked all vision, Philip lacked all hope.

Looking into the eyes of the hungry crowd, Philip saw only the empty baskets. Looking into the eyes of the hungry crowd, Philip saw only the bare cupboard. 'Jesus,' he moaned, 'how about their supper, those poor, cold, hungry, weary people? We've nothing to give them – nothing – not a crumb!' Put under pressure, Philip lacked all vision, Philip lacked all hope.

Put under pressure, Andrew quickly rose to the occasion. Put under pressure, Andrew quickly spotted the possibilities. Put under pressure, Andrew became a disciple of vision, Andrew became a disciple of hope.

Looking into the eyes of the despairing Philip, Andrew flatly refused to share his despair. 'What a fellow you are for giving in!' said Andrew reproachfully. 'What a fellow you are for giving in!'

Looking into the eyes of the despairing Philip, Andrew looked right through the despair to the very solution itself. 'Why only just now I saw a boy who has five loaves of barley bread and two small fishes; and everybody knows that this is more than enough for a miracle in the hands of the Christ.' And a miracle there was. The people were fed. Put under pressure, Philip became a disciple of vision, Philip became a prophet of hope.

You and I are given the choice to become a Rat or a Mole, a Philip or an Andrew. Pray that we may choose wisely.

PRAYER

Lord Jesus Christ,
you call your disciples
to be people of vision, people of hope.
Give us grace to see the resources around us,
vision to hand those resources to you,
and hope in your power to transform them.
For you are our God,
now and always.

Amen.

# CHAPTER SIX

# Shaping the future
# with Mr Toad

# Episode 26:
# Early morning encounter

*Scripture says that Mary Magdalene turned towards Jesus and said in Hebrew, 'Rabboni!'*

MR TOAD

It was a bright morning in the early part of summer; the river had resumed its wonted banks and its accustomed pace, and a hot sun seemed to be pulling everything green and bushy and spiky up out of the earth towards him, as if by strings. The Mole and the Water Rat had been up since dawn, very busy on matters connected with boats and the opening of the boating season; painting and varnishing, mending paddles, repairing cushions, hunting for missing boathooks, and so on; and were finishing breakfast in their little parlour and eagerly discussing their plans for the day, when a heavy knock sounded at the door.

'Bother!' said the Rat, all over egg. 'See who it is, Mole, like a good chap, since you've finished.'

The Mole went to attend the summons, and the Rat heard him utter a cry of surprise. Then he flung the parlour door open, and announced with much importance, 'Mr Badger!'

JOHN 20:11 – 16

Mary stood crying outside the tomb. While she was still crying she bent over and looked in the tomb and saw two angels there dressed in white, sitting where the body of Jesus had been, one at the head and the other at the feet. 'Woman, why are you crying?' they asked her.

She answered, 'They have taken my Lord away, and I do not know where they have put him!'

Then she turned round and saw Jesus standing there; but she did not know that it was Jesus. 'Woman, why are you crying?' Jesus asked her. 'Who is it that you are looking for?'

She thought he was the gardener, so she said to him, 'If you took him away, sir, tell me where you have put him, and I will go and get him.'

Jesus said to her, 'Mary!'

She turned towards him and said in Hebrew, 'Rabboni!' (This means 'Teacher'.)

MEDITATION

It was bright morning, and bright mornings carry hope. According to the tradition, the Mole and the Water Rat had been up since dawn. They had made an early start and were brimful with hope. It was a bright, bright morning.

It was a busy morning, and busy mornings look forward with contentment to a good job well completed. The Mole and the Water Rat had been very very busy on matters connected with boats and the opening of the boating season. It was a busy, busy morning.

It was a morning rich with aromas and smells, and rich aromas promised sensations of satisfaction. Around the

Mole and the Water Rat, the air was rich with smells of varnish and of paint, as they prepared materials for the day's work. It was a morning rich, rich with aromas and smells.

It was a morning in the early part of summer, and the early part of summer promises growth and new life. Everywhere a hot sun seemed to be pulling everything green and bushy and spiky up out of the earth, as if by strings. It was a morning in the early, early part of summer.

It was a morning clearly shaped in the minds of the Mole and the Water Rat. They knew what they expected and clearly they did not expect the unexpected to happen. It was a morning clearly, clearly shaped in the minds of the Mole and the Water Rat.

But, then, the unexpected happened. While the animals were still discussing their plans for the day, the sudden knock sounded at the door of the Rat's home. The door was thrown open and recognition was instantaneous. 'Mr Badger!' announced the Mole, with much importance.

It was a bright morning when Mr Badger turned the Mole's world upside down.

It was a bright morning, but this bright morning carried no hope. According to Mark's account, Mary Magdalene, Mary the mother of James, and Salome had been up since before dawn. They had made an early start, but they had set out without hope. It was a bright, bright morning.

It was a busy morning, but this busy morning looked forward with no contentment to a good job well completed. Mary Magdalene, Mary the mother of James, and Salome had been very very busy on matters connected with burial and the closing fast of the tomb. It was a busy, busy morning.

It was a morning rich with aromas and smells, but these aromas promised no sensations of satisfaction. Around Mary Magdalene, Mary the mother of James, and Salome, the air was rich with the smells of spices and ointment, as they prepared materials for the day's work. It was a morning rich, rich with aromas and smells.

It was a morning in the early part of summer, but this early part of summer promised no growth, promised no new life. Everywhere a hot sun seemed to be burning up and scorching everything green and bushy and spiky, destroying it from the earth, as if by tongues of fire. It was a morning in the early, early part of summer.

It was a morning clearly shaped in the minds of Mary Magdalene, Mary the mother of James, and Salome. They knew what they expected and they clearly did not expect the unexpected to happen. It was a morning clearly, clearly shaped in the minds of Mary Magdalene, Mary the mother of James, and Salome.

But, then, the unexpected happened. While the women were still discussing their plans for the day, the sudden knock sounded at the door of Mary's heart. The door was thrown open and recognition was instantaneous. 'Rabboni!' announced Mary Magdalene, with much confidence.

It was a bright morning when the risen Lord turned Mary Magdalene's world upside down.

PRAYER
Risen Lord,
you spoke Mary's name
and changed her world.
Open our ears to your voice
and give us grace to hear
you speak our name.
For you are our God,
now and always.

Amen.

# Episode 27:
# Unexpected visitor

*Scripture says that Jesus came and stood among the disciples. 'Peace be with you!' he said.*

MR TOAD

This was a wonderful thing, indeed, that the Badger should pay a formal call on them, or indeed on anybody. He generally had be to caught, if you wanted him badly, as he slipped quietly along a hedgerow of an early morning or late evening, or else hunted up in his own house in the middle of the wood, which was a serious undertaking.

The Badger strode heavily into the room, and stood looking at the two animals with an expression full of seriousness. The Rat let his egg-spoon fall on the tablecloth, and sat open-mouthed.

'The hour has come!' said the Badger at last with great solemnity.

'What hour?' asked the Rat uneasily, glancing at the clock on the mantelpiece.

'*Whose* hour, you should rather say,' replied the Badger. 'Why, Toad's hour! The hour of Toad! I said I would take him in hand as soon as the winter was well over, and I'm going to take him in hand to-day!'

'Toad's hour, of course!' cried the Mole delightedly. 'Hooray! I remember now! *We'll* teach him to be a sensible Toad!'

## JOHN 20:24 – 29

One of the twelve disciples, Thomas (called the Twin), was not with them when Jesus came. So the other disciples told him, 'We have seen the Lord!'

Thomas said to them, 'Unless I see the scars of the nails in his hands and put my finger on those scars and my hand in his side, I will not believe.'

A week later the disciples were together again indoors, and Thomas was with them. The doors were locked, but Jesus came and stood among them and said, 'Peace be with you.' Then he said to Thomas, 'Put your finger here, and look at my hands; then stretch out your hand and put it in my side. Stop your doubting, and believe!'

Thomas answered him, 'My Lord and my God!'

Jesus said to him, 'Do you believe because you see me? How happy are those who believe without seeing me!'

## MEDITATION

The Badger could be the most elusive of creatures. When his friends went seeking him, he eluded their gaze. When his friends tried to catch him, he eluded their grasp. When his friends tried to pin him down, he slipped through their net. The Badger could be the most elusive of creatures.

The Badger could be the most independent of creatures. When his friends weren't seeking him, he appeared before their eyes. When his friends weren't trying to catch him, he fell into their grasp. When his friends weren't trying to pin him down, he fell into their net. The Badger could be the most independent of creatures.

The Badger could be the most demanding of creatures. When his friends weren't seeking him, he walked into their lives. When his friends weren't trying to catch him, he demanded their attention. When his friends weren't trying to pin him down, he changed their plans. The Badger could be the most demanding of creatures.

The Badger could be the most challenging of creatures. When his friends weren't seeking him, he proclaimed, 'The hour has come!' When his friends weren't trying to catch him, he challenged them to consider the urgency of the moment. When his friends weren't trying to pin him down, he confronted them with the decisions of life. The Badger could be the most challenging of creatures.

After that first Easter morning, the risen Christ could be the most elusive of creatures. When his friends went seeking him, he eluded their gaze. When his friends tried to catch him, he eluded their grasp. When his friends tried to pin him down, he slipped through their net. The risen Christ could be the most elusive of creatures.

After that first Easter morning, the risen Christ could be the most independent of creatures. When his friends weren't seeking him, he suddenly appeared with them behind locked doors in the upper room. When his friends weren't trying to catch him, he suddenly joined them on their trek of the Emmaus road. When his friends weren't trying to pin him down, he suddenly arrived as a stranger on the shore. The risen Christ could be the most elusive of creatures.

After that first Easter morning, the risen Christ could

be the most demanding of creatures. When his friends weren't seeking him, he invited them to feel his wounds for themselves. When his friends weren't trying to catch him, he asked them to prepare the supper table. When his friends weren't trying to pin him down, he told them to cast their net on the other side. The risen Christ could be the most independent of creatures.

After that first Easter morning, the risen Christ could be the most challenging of creatures. When his friends weren't seeking him, he challenged their fear. 'Peace be with you!' he said. When his friends weren't trying to catch him, he unwrapped for them the secrets of scripture. 'How foolish you are, how slow you are to believe everything the prophet said!' he declaimed. When his friends weren't trying to pin him down, he opened their eyes to his presence and power. 'Bring some of the fish you have just caught. Come and eat!' he said. The risen Christ could be the most challenging of creatures.

PRAYER
Risen Lord,
you came to your disciples
when they least expected you.
Help us to expect
your unexpected presence
every moment of the day.
We make our prayer in your name.

Amen.

# Episode 28:
# Proclaiming salvation

*Jesus said, 'Go, then, to all peoples everywhere and make them my disciples.'*

MR TOAD

'This very morning,' continued the Badger, taking an arm-chair, 'as I learnt last night from a trustworthy source, another new and exceptionally powerful motorcar will arrive at Toad Hall on approval or return. At this very moment, perhaps, Toad is busily arraying himself in those singularly hideous habiliments so dear to him, which transform him from a (comparatively) good-looking Toad into an Object which throws any decent-minded animal that comes across it into a violent fit. We must be up and doing, ere it is too late. You two animals will accompany me instantly to Toad Hall, and the work of rescue shall be accomplished.'

'Right you are!' cried the Rat, starting up. 'We'll rescue the poor unhappy animal! We'll convert him! He'll be the most converted Toad that ever was before we've done with him!'

They set off up the road on their mission of mercy, Badger leading the way. …

They reached the carriage-drive of Toad Hall to find,

as the Badger had anticipated, a shiny new motorcar, of great size.... As they neared the door it was flung open, and Mr Toad, arrayed in goggles, cap, gaiters, and enormous overcoat, came swaggering down the steps, drawing on his gauntleted gloves.

'Hullo! come on, you fellows!' he cried cheerfully on catching sight of them. 'You're just in time to come with me for a jolly — to come for a jolly — for a — er — jolly — '

His hearty accents faltered and fell away as he noticed the stern unbending look on the countenances of his silent friends, and his invitation remained unfinished.

MATTHEW 28:16 – 20
The eleven disciples went to the hill in Galilee where Jesus had told them to go. When they saw him, they worshipped him, even though some of them doubted. Jesus drew near and said to them, 'I have been given all authority in heaven and on earth. Go, then, to all peoples everywhere and make them my disciples: baptize them in the name of the Father, the Son, and the Holy Spirit, and teach them to obey everything I have commanded you. And I will be with you always, to the end of the age.'

MEDITATION
Following the Badger's exhortation, the Mole and the Rat were animals with a missionary zeal. They were more than aware that time was short. 'We must be up and doing, ere it is too late,' the one said to the other, and the work began.

Following the Badger's exhortation, the Mole and the Rat were animals with a missionary zeal. They were more than aware of the urgency of their task. Already the Toad was busily arraying himself in garments able to transform a (comparatively) good-looking Toad into an object that throws any decent-minded animal that comes across it into a violent fit.

Following the Badger's exhortation, the Mole and the Rat were animals with a missionary zeal. They were more than aware that they were on a mission of mercy to a fallen Mr Toad. 'You will accompany me instantly, and the work of rescue shall be accomplished,' the one said to the other, and the work began.

Following the Badger's exhortation, the Mole and the Rat were animals with a missionary zeal. They were more than aware of the aim of their mission. 'We will rescue the poor unhappy animal! We will convert him! He'll be the most converted Toad that ever was before we've done with him!' the one said to the other, and the work began. The Mole and the Rat were animals with a missionary zeal.

Following the ascension of their risen Lord, the early disciples were disciples with a missionary zeal. They were more than aware that the time was short before the Lord returned. 'We must be up and doing, ere it is too late,' the one said to the other, and the work began.

Following the ascension of their risen Lord, the early disciples were disciples with a missionary zeal. They were more than aware of the urgency of their task. Already the initiatives of darkness that had crucified their master were planning to persecute the young and growing Church.

Following the ascension of their risen Lord, the early disciples were disciples with a missionary zeal. They were more than aware that they were on a mission of mercy to a fallen human race. 'You will accompany me instantly, and the work of rescue shall begin,' the one said to the other, and the work began.

Following the ascension of their risen Lord, the early disciples were disciples with a missionary zeal. They were more than aware of the aim of their mission. 'We will baptize peoples everywhere, in the name of the Father and of the Son and of the Holy Spirit, and make them Christ's disciples,' the one said to the other, and the work began. The early disciples were disciples with a missionary zeal.

You and I follow in the footsteps of the Mole and the Rat, in the footsteps of the early disciples. Pray that we may not lack their missionary zeal. Pray, at the same time, that we may treat our fellow human beings with the respect and the sensitivity that they deserve. Then, indeed, the world may be converted to faith in him who was dead and is alive.

PRAYER
Ascended Lord,
you sent your disciples
to proclaim the good news of
resurrection to all people.
Send us out in your name
to share in the work of the gospel;
to your praise and glory.

Amen.

# Episode 29:
# Facing temptation

*Jesus said, 'The gate to hell is wide and the
road that leads to it is easy.'*

MR TOAD

'There cannot be any harm,' Toad said to himself, 'in my
only just *looking* at it!'

The car stood in the middle of the yard, quite
unattended, the stable-helps and other hangers-on being
all at their dinner. Toad walked slowly round it, inspect-
ing, criticizing, musing deeply.

'I wonder,' he said to himself presently, 'I wonder if
this sort of car *starts* easily?'

Next moment, hardly knowing how it came about, he
found he had hold of the handle and was turning it. As
the familiar sound broke forth, the old passion seized on
Toad and completely mastered him, body and soul. As if
in a dream he found himself, somehow, seated in the
driver's seat; as if in a dream, he pulled the lever and
swung the car round the yard and out through the
archway; and, as if in a dream, all sense of right and
wrong, all fear of obvious consequences, seemed
temporarily suspended. He increased his pace, and as the
car devoured the street and leapt forth on the high road

through the open country, he was only conscious that he was Toad once more, Toad at his best and highest, Toad the terror, the traffic-queller, the Lord of the lone trail, before whom all must give way or be smitten into nothingness and everlasting night. He chanted as he flew, and the car responded with sonorous drone; the miles were eaten up under him as he sped he knew not whither, fulfilling his instincts, living his hour, reckless of what might come to him.

## MATTHEW 7:13 – 14

Jesus said, 'Go in through the narrow gate, because the gate to hell is wide and the road that leads to it is easy, and there are many who travel it. But the gate to life is narrow and the way that leads to it is hard, and there are few people who find it.'

## MEDITATION

The Toad was clearly obsessed by everything to do with cars. 'There cannot be any harm,' Toad said to himself, 'in my only just *looking* at it!' And so Toad went to look. He looked at the car as it stood in the middle of the yard, quite unattended.

The Toad was clearly obsessed by everything to do with cars. 'There cannot be any harm,' Toad said to himself, 'in my just *touching* it!' And so Toad went to touch. He touched the car as it stood in the middle of the yard, quite unattended.

The Toad was clearly obsessed by everything to do with cars. 'There cannot be any harm,' Toad said to himself, 'in my just *listening* to the engine!' And so Toad found he had hold of the handle and was turning it. He listened to the sound of the engine as it stood in the middle of the yard, quite unattended.

The Toad was clearly obsessed by everything to do with cars. 'There cannot be any harm,' Toad said to himself, 'in my just *sitting* in the driving seat!' And so Toad found himself, somehow, seated in the driving seat. He sat in the driving seat of the car as it stood in the middle of the yard, quite unattended.

The Toad was clearly obsessed by everything to do with cars. 'There cannot be any harm,' Toad said to himself, 'in my only just *pulling* the lever and *turning* the wheel.' And so Toad found he had selected a gear and turned a corner. And the car no longer stood in the middle of the yard, quite unattended.

The Toad drove out through the wide gate and along the wide road.

Deep down inside each of us is our own peculiar obsession, which can erode our moral judgement. Pray that, when tempted, we may choose the narrow gate.

The Toad was clearly seized by a deep deep passion that completely mastered him body and soul. As if in a dream, he found himself just *looking* at the car, and being transported into a world devoid of all notions of right and wrong.

The Toad was clearly seized by a deep deep passion that completely mastered him body and soul. As if in a dream, he found himself just *touching* the car, and being transported into a world devoid of all fear of obvious consequences.

The Toad was clearly seized by a deep deep passion that completely mastered him body and soul. As if in a dream, he found himself swinging the starting handle, *listening* to the engine, and being transported into a world devoid of all sense of responsibility and accountability.

The Toad was clearly seized by a deep deep passion that completely mastered him body and soul. As if in a dream, he found himself *sitting* in the driving seat, and being transported into a world devoid of all fear of prosecution and punishment.

The Toad was clearly seized by a deep deep passion that completely mastered him body and soul. As if in a dream, he found himself *pulling* a lever, turning a corner, and being transported into the inner world of fantasy.

Toad drove out through the wide wide gate and along the wide wide road.

Deep down inside each of us is the peculiar passion that can master body and soul. Pray that, when tempted, we may choose the narrow gate.

PRAYER
Lord Jesus Christ,
you invite us to choose
the narrow path that leads to life with you.
Give us strength to overcome
the obsessions and the passions
that lead us along the wide road away from you.
For you are our God,
now and always.

Amen.

# Episode 30:
# Facing judgement

*Jesus said, 'The King will say to the people on his left, "Away from me, you that are under God's curse!"'*

MR TOAD

'To my mind,' observed the Chairman of the Bench of Magistrates cheerfully, 'the *only* difficulty that presents itself in this otherwise very clear case is, how we can possibly make it sufficiently hot for the incorrigible rogue and hardened ruffian whom we see cowering in the dock before us. Let me see: he has been found guilty, on the clearest evidence, first, of stealing a valuable motorcar; secondly, of driving to the public danger; and, thirdly, of gross impertinence to the rural police. Mr Clerk, will you tell us, please, what is the very stiffest penalty we can impose for each of these offences? Without, of course, giving the prisoner the benefit of any doubt, because there isn't any.'

The Clerk scratched his nose with his pen. 'Some people would consider,' he observed, 'that stealing the motorcar was the worst offence; and so it is. But cheeking the police undoubtedly carries the severest penalty; and so it ought. Supposing you were to say twelve months for the theft, which is mild; and three years for the furious driving, which is lenient; and fifteen years for the cheek, which was pretty bad sort of cheek, judging by what we've heard from the witness-box, even if you only believe one-tenth part of what you heard, and I never believe more myself – those figures, if added together correctly, tot up to nineteen years '

'First rate!' said the Chairman.

'So you had better make it a round twenty years and be on the safe side,' concluded the Clerk.

'An excellent suggestion!' said the Chairman approvingly.

## MATTHEW 25:31 – 36 AND 41 – 43

Jesus said, 'When the Son of Man comes as King and all the angels with him, he will sit on his royal throne, and the people of all the nations will be gathered before him. Then he will divide them into two groups, just as a shepherd separates the sheep from the goats. He will put the righteous people on his right and the others on his left. Then the King will say to the people on his right, "Come, you that are blessed by my Father! Come and possess the kingdom which has been prepared for you ever since the creation of the world. I was hungry and you fed me, thirsty and you gave me a drink; I was a stranger and you received me in your homes, naked and you clothed me; I was sick and you took care of me, in prison and you visited me."

'Then he will say to those on his left, "Away from me, you that are under God's curse! Away to the eternal fire which has been prepared for the Devil and his angels! I was hungry but you would not feed me, thirsty but you would not give me a drink; I was a stranger but you would not welcome me in your homes, naked but you would not clothe me; I was sick and in prison but you would not take care of me.'"

MEDITATION

The Toad, you see, had been found guilty, found guilty on the clearest evidence. The Toad had been found guilty of stealing a valuable motorcar. For this defendant there is no benefit of any doubt, because there isn't any doubt.

The Toad, you see, had been found guilty, found guilty on the clearest evidence. The Toad had been found guilty of driving to the public danger. For this defendant there is no benefit of any doubt, because there isn't any doubt.

The Toad, you see, had been found guilty, found guilty on the clearest evidence. The Toad had been found guilty of gross impertinence to the rural police. For this defendant there is no benefit of any doubt, because there isn't any doubt.

The goats, too, on the King's left had been found guilty, found guilty on the clearest evidence. The goats had been found guilty of offering no food to the hungry, guilty of offering no drink to the thirsty. For these defendants there is no benefit of any doubt, because there isn't any doubt.

The goats, you see, on the King's left had been found guilty, found guilty on the clearest evidence. The goats had been found guilty of offering no welcome to the stranger, guilty of offering no clothing to the naked. For these defendants there is no benefit of any doubt, because there isn't any doubt.

The goats, you see, on the King's left had been found

guilty, found guilty on the clearest evidence. The goats had been found guilty of offering no nursing to the sick, of offering no caring to the prisoner. For these defendants there is no benefit of any doubt, because there isn't any doubt.

The Chairman of the Bench of Magistrates, you see, showed no mercy. 'The only difficulty that presents itself,' said the Chairman of the Bench, 'is how we can possibly make it sufficiently hot for the incorrigible Mr Toad.' Otherwise the case is very clear.

The Chairman of the Bench of Magistrates, you see, showed no mercy. 'Let me see,' said the Chairman of the Bench, 'the Toad has been found guilty on the clearest evidence, first, of stealing a valuable motorcar; secondly, of driving to the public danger; and, thirdly, of gross impertinence to the rural police.' The case is perfectly clear.

'So you had better make it a round twenty years and be on the safe side,' concluded the clerk.

The King of all the angels, too, will show no mercy. 'The only difficulty that presents itself,' said the King of all the angels, 'is how we can possibly make it sufficiently hot for the incorrigible goats.' Otherwise the case is very clear.

The King of all the angels, you see, will show no mercy. 'Let me see,' said the King of all the angels. 'The goats have been found guilty on the clearest evidence, first, of failing to feed the hungry and to give drink to the thirsty; secondly, of offering no welcome to the stranger and no clothing to the naked; and, thirdly, of offering no nursing to the sick and no caring to the prisoner.' The case is perfectly clear.

'So you had better make it a round eternity and be on

the safe side,' concluded the judgemental Matthew.

Pray that the Lord, whom we love and serve, may be more generous to us than the Chairman of the Bench of Magistrates; that he may be more generous to us than the King of all the angels; that he may be more generous to us than we ourselves deserve.

PRAYER
Almighty God, heavenly King,
you know our failings
and you know the judgement we deserve.
We pray you to forgive our failings
and to show us the mercy we do not deserve;
through Jesus Christ
who died for our sins.

Amen.

CHAPTER SEVEN

# The piper at the
# gates of heaven

# Episode 31: The lost son

*Jesus said, 'The younger son sold his part of the property and left home with the money.'*

THE PIPER

'Mole,' said the Rat, 'I'm afraid Otter is in trouble. Little Portly is missing again; and you know what a lot his father thinks of him, though he never says much about it.'

'What, that child?' said the Mole lightly. 'Well, suppose he is; why worry about it? He's always straying off and getting lost, and turning up again; he's so adventurous. But no harm ever happens to him. Everybody hereabouts knows him and likes him, just as they do old Otter, and you may be sure some animal or other will come across him and bring him back again all right. Why, we've found him ourselves, miles from home, and quite self-possessed and cheerful!'

'Yes; but this time it's more serious,' said the Rat gravely. 'He's been missing for some days now, and the Otters have hunted everywhere, high and low, without finding the slightest trace. And they've asked every animal, too, for miles around, and no one knows anything about him. Otter's evidently more anxious than he'll admit. I got out of him that young Portly hasn't learnt to swim very well yet, and I can see he's thinking of the weir.

There's a lot of water coming down still, considering the time of year, and the place always had a fascination for the child. And then there are – well, traps and things – *you* know.'

## LUKE 15:11 – 16

Jesus went on to say, 'There was once a man who had two sons. The younger one said to him, "Father, give me my share of the property now." So the man divided his property between his two sons. After a few days the younger son sold his part of the property and left home with the money. He went to a country far away, where he wasted his money in reckless living. He spent everything he had. Then a severe famine spread over that country, and he was left without a thing. So he went to work for one of the citizens of that country, who sent him out to his farm to take care of the pigs. He wished he could fill himself with the bean pods the pigs ate, but no one gave him anything to eat.'

## MEDITATION

Sometimes leaving home can be more difficult for those who are left behind than for those who get up and go. Of course, we do not know for sure from the story itself, but there is little to suggest in the narrative that little Portly even thought twice about getting up and going. Yesterday he was there at home, and today he is gone. Yesterday his bed was occupied, and today his bed is empty. But it must have been hard on the old old Otter.

Sometimes letting others leave home can be more difficult than getting up and going away yourself. Of course, we do not know for sure from the story itself, but there is little to suggest in the narrative that the Otter did anything to stand in the way of little Portly's freedom to go as he chose. But it must have been hard on the old old Otter.

Sometimes keeping faith with those who get up and walk away from home can be more difficult than standing by those who remain firmly at home. Of course, we do not know for sure from the story itself, but there is little to suggest in the narrative that the Otter showed any sign of resentment or anger at little Portly's departure. But it must have been hard on the old old Otter.

Sometimes keeping the bed aired and keeping the door open for the prodigal's return can be more difficult than turning round and heading back for home. Of course, we do not know for sure from the story itself, but there is little to suggest in the narrative that the Otter thought of anything other than welcoming little Portly back home from the very moment that he left. But it must have been hard on the old old Otter.

Sometimes leaving home can be more difficult for those who are left behind than for those who get up and go. Of course, Jesus never spelt it out in the parable, but there is little to suggest in the text itself that the younger son even thought twice about getting up and going. Yesterday he was at home, and today he is gone. Yesterday his bed was occupied, and today his bed is empty. But it must have been hard on the old old father.

Sometimes letting others leave home can be more difficult than getting up and going away yourself. Of course, Jesus never spelt it out in the parable, but there is little to suggest in the text itself that the father did anything to stand in the way of the younger son's freedom to go as he chose. But it must have been hard on the old old father.

Sometimes keeping faith with those who get up and

walk away from home can be more difficult than standing by those who remain firmly at home. Of course, Jesus never spelt it out in the parable, but there is little to suggest in the text itself that the father showed any sign of resentment or anger at the younger son's departure. But it must have been hard on the old old father.

Sometimes keeping the bed aired and keeping the door open for the prodigal's return can be more difficult than turning round and heading back for home. Of course, Jesus never spelt it out in the parable, but there is little to suggest in the text itself that the father thought of anything other than welcoming the younger son back home from the very moment that he left. But it must have been hard on the old old father.

Like little Portly, and like the younger son, you and I are prone to wander from the home of our God in heaven. Like the old old Otter and like the old old father, our God in heaven awaits our return, with a warm hearth, outstretched arms and a welcoming heart.

PRAYER
God in heaven,
you give us freedom to leave your home
and yet you wait to welcome our return.
Give us grace to recognise your welcome
and to receive your gift of forgiveness.
We make our prayer in Jesus' name.

Amen.

# Episode 32: Keeping watch

*Jesus said, 'Keep watch with me.'*

THE PIPER

'When I left,' said the Rat, 'Otter came out with me –
said he wanted some air, and talked about stretching his
legs. But I could see it wasn't that, so I drew him out and
pumped him, and got it all from him at last. He was going
to spend the night watching by the ford. ... Otter goes
there every night and watches – on the chance, you
know, just on the chance!'

They were silent for a time, both thinking of the same
thing – the lonely, heart-sore animal, crouched by the
ford, watching and waiting, the long night through – on
the chance.

'Well, well,' said the Rat presently, 'I suppose we
ought to be thinking about turning in.' But he never
offered to move.

'Rat,' said the Mole, 'I simply can't go and turn in, and
go to sleep, and *do* nothing, even though there doesn't
seem to be anything to be done. We'll get the boat out,
and paddle upstream. The moon will be up in an hour or
so, and then we will search as well as we can – anyhow,
it will be better than going to bed and doing *nothing*.'

'Just what I was thinking myself,' said the Rat. 'It's not
the sort of night for bed anyhow.'

MATTHEW 26:36 – 41

Then Jesus went with his disciples to a place called Gethsemane, and he said to them, 'Sit here while I go over there and pray.' He took with him Peter and the two sons of Zebedee. Grief and anguish came over him, and he said to them, 'The sorrow in my heart is so great that it almost crushes me. Stay here and keep watch with me.'

He went a little farther on, threw himself face downwards on the ground, and prayed, 'My Father, if it is possible, take this cup of suffering from me! Yet not what I want, but what you want.'

Then he returned to the three disciples and found them asleep; and he said to Peter, 'How is it that you three were not able to keep watch with me even for one hour? Keep watch and pray that you will not fall into temptation. The spirit is willing, but the flesh is weak.'

MEDITATION

Keeping watch is no easy matter. The Otter knew that the hours of darkness would be cold and long, out there watching by the ford. The Otter knew that throughout the darkness he would be alone and lonely. And yet the Otter knew that he had no choice but to wait and to watch. The Otter knew that he had no choice but to wait and to watch the long night through, on the chance that little Portly might pass that way. Keeping watch is no easy matter.

Knowing that others are keeping watch is no easy matter. The Rat went away uneasy, with the Otter's words ringing still in his ears. The Rat went away uneasy, knowing that the Otter was committed to his long, solitary, nocturnal vigil, waiting and watching for the dawn to come. The Rat went away uneasy knowing that his friend was ill at ease. Knowing that others are keeping watch is no easy matter.

Supporting those who are keeping watch is no easy matter. The Rat felt so powerless. The Rat felt so helpless. The Rat felt so useless. 'Well, well,' said the Rat presently. 'I suppose we ought to think about turning in.' Well, what else could the Rat say; what else could the Rat do under the circumstances? Supporting those who are keeping watch is no easy matter.

And, yet, in spite of his uncertainty, the Rat went out into the cold dark night and was there, there by the riverbank when he was needed most.

Keeping watch is no easy matter. Jesus knew that the hours of darkness would be cold and long, out there watching in the garden of Gethsemane. Jesus knew that throughout the darkness he would be alone and lonely. And yet Jesus knew that he had no choice but to wait and to watch. Jesus knew that he had no choice but to wait and to watch the long night through, on the chance that the cup of suffering might pass from him. Keeping watch is no easy matter.

Knowing that others are keeping watch is no easy matter. Peter, James and John felt uneasy, as Jesus went away leaving his words ringing still in their ears. Peter, James and John felt uneasy, knowing that Jesus was committed to his long, solitary, nocturnal vigil, waiting and watching for the dawn to come. Peter, James and John felt uneasy knowing that their friend was ill at ease. Knowing that others are keeping watch is no easy matter.

Supporting those who are keeping watch is no easy matter. Peter, James and John felt so powerless. Peter, James and John felt so helpless. Peter, James and John felt so useless. 'Well, well,' said Peter, James and John presently. 'I suppose we ought to be thinking about turning in.' Well, what else could the disciples say; what else could the disciples do under the circumstances? Supporting those who are keeping watch is no easy matter.

And, yet, in spite of their uncertainty, Peter, James and John went out into the cold dark night and were there, there in the garden when they were needed most.

Pray, then, that, like the Rat and like Peter, James and John, you and I may keep watch when we are most called upon to do so.

PRAYER
Lord Jesus Christ,
you invited your followers
to keep watch during your time of need.
Give us strength to watch
with those who need your care and support.
For you are our Lord,
now and always.

Amen.

# Episode 33: Keep looking

*Jesus says, 'The woman looks carefully everywhere until she finds it.'*

THE PIPER

Fastening their boat to a willow, the Mole and the Rat landed in this silent, silver kingdom, and patiently explored the hedges, the hollow trees, the runnels and their little culverts, the ditches and dry water-ways. Embarking again and crossing over, they worked their way up the stream in this manner, while the moon, serene and detached in a cloudless sky, did what she could, though so far off, to help them in their quest; till her hour came and she sank earthwards reluctantly, and left them, and mystery once more held field and river.

Then a change began slowly to declare itself. The horizon became clearer, field and tree came more into sight, and somehow with a different look; the mystery began to drop away from them. A bird piped suddenly, and was still; and a light breeze sprang up and set the reeds and bulrushes rustling. Rat, who was in the stern of the boat, while Mole sculled, sat up suddenly and listened with a passionate intentness. Mole, who with gentle strokes was just keeping the boat moving while he scanned the banks with care, looked at him with curiosity.

'It's gone!' sighed the Rat, sinking back in his seat again. 'So beautiful and strange and new! Since it was to end so soon, I almost wish I had never heard it. For it has roused a longing in me that is pain, and nothing seems worthwhile but just to hear that sound once more and go on listening to it for ever. No! There it is again!' he cried, alert once more. Entranced, he was silent for a long space, spellbound.

'Now it passes on and I begin to lose it,' he said presently. 'O, Mole! the beauty of it! The merry bubble and joy, the thin, clear happy call of the distant piping! Such music I never dreamed of, and the call in it is stronger even than the music is sweet! Row on, Mole, row! For the music and the call must be for us.'

LUKE 15:8 – 9

Jesus said, 'Suppose a woman who has ten silver coins loses one of them – what does she do? She lights a lamp, sweeps her house, and looks carefully everywhere until she finds it. When she finds it, she calls her friends and neighbours together, and says to them, 'I am so happy I found the coin I lost. Let us celebrate!'

MEDITATION

The Mole and the Rat had had a hard hard time of it. They looked and they looked and they looked. They began looking by patiently exploring the hedges, the hollow trees, the runnels and their little culverts, the ditches and the dry waterways. They looked this way and that way. They looked up stream and down stream. They looked and they looked and they saw nothing, nothing.

The Mole and the Rat had a hard hard time of it. They looked and they looked and they looked. They slowly worked their way up the stream looking and looking and looking, while the moon, serene and detached in the cloudless sky, did what she could, though far off, to help them in their quest. They looked and they looked and they saw nothing, nothing.

Then, suddenly, there was the first clue, the first distant whisper, the first promise of success. Their spirits lifted and they began to celebrate.

The woman who now has nine silver coins had had a hard hard time of it. She looked and she looked and she looked. She began looking by patiently exploring the cupboards and the drawers, the pots and pans, the mat and the floor under the mat. She looked this way and that way. She looked upstairs and downstairs. She looked and she looked and she saw nothing, nothing.

The woman who now has nine silver coins had had a hard hard time of it. She looked and she looked and she looked. She slowly worked her way around the house looking and looking and looking, while the specially lighted lamp, bright and flickering, did what it could, to help the woman in her quest. She looked and she looked and she saw nothing, nothing.

Then, suddenly, there was the first clue, the first distant glimmer of silver, the first promise of success. Her spirits lifted and she began to celebrate.

Ever since the primordial act of human disobedience, your God in heaven has had a hard hard time of it. Your God in heaven has looked and looked and looked for the sinner who is repentant. Your God in heaven has searched the hillside for the lost sheep. Your God in heaven has searched the hearthside for the lost coin. Your God in heaven has roamed the riverbank waiting for the lost son's return.

Then, there is the first clue of repentance, the first distant whisper of penitence, the first grasp towards salvation. And your God in heaven calls us to share in the joy and the celebration.

Pray, then, that, like the Rat, you may hear the distant music of celebration, when your God in heaven calls you to rejoice with the lost who are found. Pray, then, that, like the woman who now has ten silver coins, you may call others to share in the celebration that your God in heaven initiates.

PRAYER
Lord God,
you search patiently for those who are lost
and rejoice greatly when they are found.
Give your Church grace
to proclaim salvation to the lost
and to share your joy of celebration.
For we, too, are lost,
until we are found in you.

Amen.

# Episode 34:
# Divine encounter
*Scripture says, 'The disciples were afraid.'*

THE PIPER

Then suddenly the Mole felt a great Awe fall upon him, an awe that turned his muscles to water, bowed his head, and rooted his feet to the ground. It was no panic terror – indeed he felt wonderfully at peace and happy – but it was an awe that smote and held him and, without seeing, he knew it could only mean that some august Presence was very, very near. With difficulty he turned to look for his friend, and saw him at his side cowed, stricken, and trembling violently. And still there was utter silence in the populous bird-haunted branches around them; and still the light grew and grew.

Perhaps he would never have dared to raise his eyes, but that, though the piping was now hushed, the call and the summons seemed still dominant and imperious. He might not refuse, were Death himself waiting to strike him instantly, once he had looked with mortal eye on things rightly kept hidden. Trembling he obeyed, and raised his humble head; and then, in that utter clearness of the imminent dawn, while Nature, flushed with fullness of incredible colour, seemed to hold her breath for the event, he looked in the very eyes of the Friend and Helper; saw the backward sweep of the curved horns, gleaming in the growing daylight; saw the stern, hooked nose between the kindly eyes that were looking down on them humorously, while the bearded mouth broke into a half-smile at the corners.... All this he saw, for one moment breathless and intense, vivid on the morning sky; and still, as he looked, he lived; and still, as he lived, he wondered.

'Rat!' he found breath to whisper, shaking. 'Are you afraid?'

'Afraid?' murmured the Rat, his eyes shining with unutterable love. 'Afraid! Of *Him*? O, never, never! And yet – and yet – O, Mole, I am afraid!'

Then the two animals, crouching to the earth, bowed their heads and did worship.

LUKE 9:28 – 35

About a week after he had said these things, Jesus took Peter, John, and James with him and went up a hill to pray. While he was praying, his face changed its appearance, and his clothes became dazzling white. Suddenly two men were there talking with him. They were Moses and Elijah, who appeared in heavenly glory and talked with Jesus about the way in which he would soon fulfil God's purpose by dying in Jerusalem. Peter and his companions were sound asleep, but they woke up and saw Jesus' glory and the two men who were standing with him. As the men were leaving Jesus, Peter said to him, 'Master, how good it is that we are here! We will make three tents, one for you, one for Moses, and one for Elijah.' (He did not really know what he was saying.)

While he was still speaking, a cloud appeared and covered them with its shadow; and the disciples were afraid as the cloud came over them. A voice said from the cloud, 'This is my Son, whom I have chosen – listen to him!'

MEDITATION

You see, it is not always easy to find the right words to express exactly how we feel. Sometimes the experience is just too too big and the available language is just too too small. It was a little like that for Mole, when Mole found himself there in the presence of the divine, on that island in the very heart of the river.

It is not always easy to find the right words to express exactly how it feels. But, nonetheless, the feelings are clear enough. As he stood there on that island in the very heart of the river, the Mole felt his muscles turn to water; the Mole felt his feet rooted to the ground; the Mole felt wonderfully at peace; the Mole felt wonderfully happy; the Mole felt the whole of his little body tremble with fear. Sometimes the experience is just too too big and the available language is just too too small.

It is not always easy to find the right words to express exactly how it feels. But, nonetheless, where words fail, body language speaks true. The Mole did crouch to the earth, bowed his head and worshipped. For here is the language of awe.

It is not always easy to find the right words to express exactly how it feels. When, at last, the Mole found the breath to whisper, the only word he could find was 'fear'. 'Rat!' he whispered, 'Are you afraid?' and the Rat thought carefully and thoughtfully. 'Afraid! Of *him*? O, never, never! And yet – and yet – O, Mole, I am afraid!'

Sometimes the experience is just too too big and the available language is just too too small.

You see, it is not always easy to find the right words to express exactly how it feels. Sometimes the experience is just too too big and the available language is just too too small. It was a little like that for Peter, James and John, when they found themselves there in the presence of the divine, on that mountain in the very heart of the gospel.

It is not always easy to find the right words to express exactly how it feels. But, nonetheless, the feelings are clear enough. As they stood there on that mountain in the very heart of the gospel, Peter, James and John felt their muscles turn to water; Peter, James and John felt their feet rooted to the ground; Peter, James and John felt wonderfully at peace; Peter, James and John felt wonderfully happy; Peter, James and John felt the whole of their little bodies tremble with fear. Sometimes the experience is just too too big and the available language is just too too small.

It is not always easy to find the right words to express how it feels. But, nonetheless, where words fail, body language speaks true. Peter, James and John did crouch to the earth, bowed their heads and worshipped. For here is the language of awe.

It is not always easy to find the right words to express exactly how it feels. When, at last, Peter found the breath to whisper, the only idea to which he gave expression was this: 'Master, shall we make three tents, one for you, one for Moses, and one for Elijah?' For you see, Peter was afraid. Sometimes the experience is just too too big and the available language is just too too small.

Pray, then, that you may never be tempted to limit

the breadth and depth of your experience of the divine to
that which you can put into words.

PRAYER
Lord God,
the heavens themselves cannot contain you
and human words cannot describe you.
Open our hearts to experience your presence
and liberate the language of our bodies
to express our feelings of wonder and awe;
to your praise and glory,
now and always.

Amen.

# Episode 35:
# The son restored

*The father said, 'He was lost, but now he has been found.'*

THE PIPER

The main river reached again, they turned the boat's head upstream, towards the point where they knew their friend was keeping his lonely vigil. As they drew near the familiar ford, the Mole took the boat in to the bank, and they lifted Portly out and set him on his legs on the tow-path, gave him his marching orders and a friendly farewell pat on the back, and shoved out into mid-stream. They watched the little animal as he waddled along the path contentedly and with importance; watched him till they saw his muzzle suddenly lift and his waddle break into a clumsy amble as he quickened his pace with shrill whines and wriggles of recognition. Looking up the river, they could see Otter start up, tense and rigid, from out of the shallows where he crouched in dumb patience, and could hear his amazed and joyous bark as he bounded up through the osiers on to the path. Then the Mole, with a strong pull on one oar, swung the boat round and let the full steam bear them down again whither it would, their quest now happily ended.

LUKE 15:20B – 24

Jesus continued, 'The younger son was still a long way from home when his father saw him; his heart was filled with pity, and he ran, threw his arms round his son, and kissed him. "Father," the son said, "I have sinned against God and against you. I am no longer fit to be called your son." But the father called his servants. "Hurry!" he said. "Bring the best robe and put it on him. Put a ring on his finger and shoes on his feet. Then go and get the prize calf and kill it, and let us celebrate with a feast! For this son of mine was dead, but now he is alive; he was lost, but now he has been found." And so the feasting began.'

MEDITATION

Absence, it is said, does not always make the heart grow fonder. Little Portly had been absent for a long long time. Little Portly seems to have been oblivious to the pain and to the anguish caused by his long long absence. It is by no means clear that absence had made little Portly's heart grow fonder.

Absence, it is said, does not always make the heart grow fonder. The old Otter had been waiting for a long long time. The old Otter had spent restless days and sleepless nights, keeping watch for little Portly's return. The old Otter had lamented the young Portly's absence and confided his hurt to the Rat. It is by no means clear that Portly's absence should have made the old Otter's heart grow fonder.

Absence, it is said, does not always make the heart grow fonder. The old Otter could have grown tired; the old Otter could have grown bitter; the old Otter could have felt slighted; the old Otter could have set his heart on revenge and on punishment. It is by no means clear that Portly's absence should have made the old Otter's heart grow fonder.

And yet, as soon as the old Otter saw young Portly in the distance, he bounded up onto the path with an amazed and joyous bark. 'My little Portly was lost, but now he has been found!' said the Otter. 'Come, let us celebrate with a feast!'

Absence, it is said, does not always make the heart grow fonder. The younger son had been absent for a long long time. The younger son seems to have been oblivious to the pain and to the anguish caused by his long long absence. It is by no means clear that absence had made the younger son's heart grow fonder.

Absence, it is said, does not always make the heart grow fonder. The old father had been waiting for a long long time. The old father had spent restless days and sleepless nights, keeping watch for the younger son's return. The old father had lamented the younger son's absence and confided his hurt to the fatted calf. It is by no means clear that the younger son's absence should have made the old father's heart grow fonder.

Absence, it is said, does not always make the heart grow fonder. The old father could have grown tired; the old father could have grown bitter; the old father could have felt slighted; the old father could have set his heart on revenge and on punishment. It is by no means clear that the younger son's absence should have made the old father's heart grow fonder.

And yet, as soon as the old father saw the younger son in the distance, he bounded up onto the path with an amazed and joyous shout. 'My younger son was lost, but now he has been found!' said the old father. 'Come, let us celebrate with a feast!'

Be assured, says Jesus, that your God in heaven welcomes your return. Be assured, says Jesus, that your God in heaven does not require your absence to make God's heart grow fonder. Be assured, too, that your absence does not make God's heart grow cold.

PRAYER
Lord God,
you remain faithful to your people
and rejoice when the lost ones return.
Give us confidence in your mercy
and the courage to return to you.
For you are our God,
now and always.

Amen.

## CHAPTER EIGHT

# Learning from Toad's adventures

# Episode 36: Cast into prison

*Jesus said, 'There you will stay, I tell you, until you pay the last penny of your fine.'*

TOAD'S ADVENTURES

When Toad found himself immured in a dank and noisome dungeon, and knew that all the grim darkness of a medieval fortress lay between him and the outer world of sunshine and well-metalled high roads where he had lately been so happy, disporting himself as if he had bought up every road in England, he flung himself at full length on the floor, and shed bitter tears, and abandoned himself to dark despair. 'This is the end of everything' (he said), 'at least it is the end of the career of Toad, which is the same thing; the popular and handsome Toad, the rich and hospitable Toad, the Toad so free and careless and debonair! How can I hope to be ever set at large again' (he said), 'who have been imprisoned so justly for stealing so handsome a motor-car in such an audacious manner, and for such lurid and imaginative cheek, bestowed upon such a number of fat, red-faced policemen!' (Here his sobs choked him.) 'Stupid animal that I was' (he said), 'now I must languish in this dungeon, till people who were proud to say they knew me, have forgotten the very name of Toad! O wise old Badger!' (he said), 'O clever, intelligent Rat and sensible

Mole! What sound judgements, what a knowledge of men and matters you possess!'

MATTHEW 5:21 – 26

Jesus said, 'You have heard that people were told in the past, "Do not commit murder; anyone who does will be brought to trial." But now I tell you: whoever is angry with his brother will be brought to trial, whoever calls his brother "You good-for-nothing!" will be brought before the Council, and whoever calls his brother a worthless fool will be in danger of going to the fire of hell. So if you are about to offer your gift to God at the altar and there you remember that your brother has something against you, leave your gift there in front of the altar, go at once and make peace with your brother, and then come back and offer your gift to God.

'If someone brings a lawsuit against you and takes you to court, settle the dispute with him while there is time, before you get to court. Once you are there, he will hand you over to the judge, who will hand you over to the police, and you will be put in jail. There you will stay, I tell you, until you pay the last penny of your fine.'

MEDITATION

Toad had failed to listen to good advice. Toad had failed to understand. Now Toad found himself immured in a dank and noisome dungeon. Now Toad knew that all the grim darkness of the medieval fortress lay between him and the outer world of sunshine. Toad had failed to listen to good advice. Toad had failed to understand.

Toad had heard that people were told in the past, 'Do not covet your neighbour's motor car. Do not steal your neighbour's limousine.' But Toad had failed to listen to good advice. Toad had failed to understand. Now Toad found himself cast into jail, there to stay until he paid the last penny of his justly-deserved fine.

Toad had heard that people were told in the past, 'Do not insult the constable. Do not humiliate the justice of the peace.' But Toad had failed to listen to good advice. Toad had failed to understand. Now Toad found himself cast into jail, there to stay until he paid the last penny of his justly-deserved fine.

Have you, too, failed to listen to good advice? Have you, too, failed to understand? Have you heard that people were told in the past, 'Do not commit murder. Do not kill'? For those who commit murder build around themselves prison walls as they try to hide their shame from the all-seeing eyes of God.

Have you, too, failed to listen to good advice? Have you, too, failed to understand? Have you heard that Jesus said, 'Whoever is angry with his brother or sister will be brought to trial'? For those who are angry with their fellow human beings build around themselves prison walls as they try to hide their shame from the all-seeing eyes of God.

Have you, too, failed to listen to good advice? Have you, too, failed to understand? Have you heard that Jesus said, 'Whoever calls his brother or sister "You good-for-nothing!" will be brought before the Council'? Those who insult their fellow human beings build around themselves prison walls as they try to hide their shame from the all-seeing eyes of God.

Have you, too, failed to listen to good advice? Have you, too, failed to understand? Have you heard that Jesus said, 'Whoever calls his brother a worthless fool will be in danger of going to the fire of hell'? Those who devalue their fellow human beings build around themselves prison walls as they try to hide their shame from the all-seeing eyes of God.

Toad had failed to listen to good advice. Yet, Toad did not fail to learn from experience. As the prison walls grew tall around him, Toad saw his true self in the darkness. As the prison walls hemmed him in on every side, Toad turned and repented. 'Stupid animal that I was,' he said. And repenting he recognised the wisdom of the good advice he had failed to heed.

Pray that Toad's example may inspire you to repent in the selfsame way. As the prison walls grow tall around you, see your true self in the darkness, before it is too late. As the prison walls hem you in on every side, turn and repent, stupid animal that you are, before it is too late. And repenting, recognise the wisdom of the advice that you have failed to heed.

For that act of repentance pays the last penny of your fine.

PRAYER
Lord Jesus Christ,
you taught your followers
to make peace with one another.
Give us grace to show true repentance
and deliver us from the prison walls of sin,
for your name's sake.

Amen.

# Episode 37:
# Visiting prisoners

*Jesus said, 'The King will reply, "I tell you, whenever you did this for one of the least important of these brothers of mine, you did it for me!"'*

TOAD'S ADVENTURES
Now the gaoler had a daughter, a pleasant wench and good-hearted, who assisted her father in the lighter duties of his post. She was particularly fond of animals, and, besides her canary, whose cage hung on a nail in the massive wall of the keep by day, to the great annoyance of prisoners who relished an after-dinner nap, and was shrouded in an antimacassar on the parlour table at night, she kept several piebald mice and a restless revolving squirrel. This kind-hearted girl, pitying the misery of Toad, said to her father one day, 'Father! I can't bear to see that poor beast so unhappy, and getting so thin! You let me have the managing of him. You know how fond of animals I am. I'll make him eat from my hand, and sit up, and do all sorts of things.'

Her father replied that she could do what she liked with him. He was tired of Toad, and his sulks and his airs and his meanness. So that day she went on her errand of mercy, and knocked at the door of Toad's cell.

'Now, cheer up, Toad,' she said coaxingly, on entering, 'and sit up and dry your eyes and be a sensible animal. And do try and eat a bit of dinner. See, I've brought you some of mine, hot from the oven!'

## MATTHEW 25:34 – 40

Jesus said, 'Then the King will say to the people on his right, "Come, you that are blessed by my Father! Come and possess the kingdom which has been prepared for you ever since the creation of the world. I was hungry and you fed me, thirsty and you gave me a drink; I was a stranger and you received me in your homes, naked and you clothed me; I was sick and you took care of me, in prison and you visited me."

'The righteous will then answer him, "When, Lord, did we ever see you hungry and feed you, or thirsty and give you a drink? When did we ever see you a stranger and welcome you in our homes, or naked and clothe you? When did we ever see you sick or in prison, and visit you?" The King will reply, "I tell you, whenever you did this for one of the least important of these brothers of mine, you did it for me!"'

## MEDITATION

The gaoler's daughter was a pleasant wench, a good-natured and kind-hearted girl. She took pity on the misery of Toad. 'Father!' she said, 'I can't bear to see that poor beast so unhappy, and getting so thin!'

The gaoler's daughter was a pleasant wench, a good-natured and kind-hearted girl. She saw the poor miserable Toad languishing immured within the dank and noisome prison. And she came to visit him. 'Now, cheer up, Toad,' she said coaxingly on entering. The King saw and noted in the book of life how the gaoler's daughter recognised that he was a prisoner, and came to visit him.

The gaoler's daughter was a pleasant wench, a good-natured and kind-hearted girl. She saw the poor miserable Toad growing faint and sick in a world hidden from the healing rays of sun. And she came to take care of him. 'Now, sit up and dry your eyes and be a sensible animal,' she said coaxingly on entering. The King saw and noted in the book of life how the gaoler's daughter recognised that he was sick, and came to take care of him.

The gaoler's daughter was a pleasant wench, a good-natured and kind-hearted girl. She saw the poor miserable Toad growing thin from hunger and losing all appetite for food. And she came to feed him. 'Do try and eat a bit of dinner,' she said. 'See, I've brought you some of mine, hot from the oven!' The King saw and noted in his book of life how the gaoler's daughter recognised that he was hungry, and came to feed him.

The gaoler's daughter was a pleasant wench, a good-natured and kind-hearted girl. She saw the poor miserable Toad growing parched from thirst and losing all appetite for life. And she came to give him drink. The King saw and noted in his book of life how the gaoler's daughter recognised that he was thirsty, and came to bring him drink.

The gaoler's daughter was a pleasant wench, a good-natured and kind-hearted girl. She saw the poor miserable Toad living as a disoriented stranger in an alien land. And she came to offer him welcome. 'I'll make him eat from my hand, and sit up, and do all sorts of things,' she said. The King saw and noted in his book of life how the gaoler's daughter recognised that he was a stranger in an alien land, and came to make him welcome.

The gaoler's daughter was a pleasant wench, a good-natured and kind-hearted girl. She saw the poor miserable Toad shivering naked in the cold. And she came to clothe him. 'Now cheer up, Toad,' she said on entering. The King saw and noted in his book of life how the gaoler's daughter recognised that he stood naked in the cold, and came to clothe him.

The gaoler's daughter was a pleasant wench, a good-natured and kind-hearted girl. She took pity on the misery of Toad. 'Father!' she said. I can't bear to see that poor beast so unhappy, and getting so thin!' And the King replied, 'I tell you, whenever you did this for one of the least important of these brothers or sisters of mine, you did it for me!'

And Jesus said, 'So go and do likewise!'

PRAYER
Lord Jesus Christ,
you meet us in the lives of others.
Open our eyes to see your needs
and open our hearts to respond to them,
for you are our God,
now and for ever.

Amen.

# Episode 38:
# Dreaming of home

*Jesus says, 'There are many rooms in my Father's house, and I am going to prepare a place for you.'*

TOAD'S ADVENTURES

'Tell me about Toad Hall,' said the gaoler's daughter. 'It sounds beautiful.'

'Toad Hall,' said the Toad proudly, 'is an eligible self-contained gentleman's residence, very unique; dating in part from the fourteenth century, but replete with every modern convenience. Up-to-date sanitation. Five minutes from church, post office, and golf-links. Suitable for –'

'Bless the animal,' said the girl, laughing, 'I don't want to *take* it. Tell me something *real* about it. But first wait till I fetch you some more tea and toast.'

She tripped away, and presently returned with a fresh trayful; and Toad, pitching into the toast with avidity, his spirits quite restored to their usual level, told her about the boat-house, and the fish-pond, and the old walled kitchen-garden; and about the pig-sties, and the stables, and the pigeon-house, and the hen-house; and about the dairy, and the wash-house, and the china-cupboards, and the linen-presses (she liked that bit especially); and about the banqueting-hall, and the fun they had there when the other animals were gathered round the table and Toad was at his best, singing songs, telling stories, carrying on generally.

## JOHN 14:1-6

'Do not be worried and upset,' Jesus told them. 'Believe in God and believe also in me. There are many rooms in my Father's house, and I am going to prepare a place for you. I would not tell you this if it were not so. And after I go and prepare a place for you, I will come back and take you to myself, so that you will be where I am. You know the way that leads to the place where I am going.'

Thomas said to him, 'Lord, we do not know where you are going; so how can we know the way to get there?'

Jesus answered him, 'I am the way, the truth, and the life; no one goes to the Father except by me.'

## MEDITATION

There are some things that just have to be taken on trust. But it is not always easy to grasp the detail.

'Tell me about Toad Hall,' said the gaoler's daughter. 'It sounds beautiful.' 'Toad Hall,' said the Toad proudly, 'is an eligible self-contained gentleman's residence, very unique; dating in part from the fourteenth century, but replete with every modern convenience. Up-to-date sanitation. Five minutes from church.' But the gaoler's daughter, not noted for believing everything she heard, failed to be convinced. 'Bless the animal,' said the girl, laughing. 'Tell me something *real* about it.'

Now, for the Toad, reality comprised the boat-house, and the fish-pond, and the old walled kitchen-garden; and the pig-sties, and the stables, and the pigeon-house, and the hen-house; and the dairy, and the wash-house, and the china-cupboards, and the linen-presses; and the banqueting-hall.

'Tell me something *real* about it,' demanded the gaoler's daughter. And at last Toad's well-articulated description began to convince her that there was indeed substance behind the dream. Not having seen with her own eyes, yet she begins to believe.

There are some things that just have to be taken on trust. But it is not always easy to grasp the detail.

'Tell me about your father's house,' said Thomas the doubter. 'It sounds very beautiful.' 'In my father's house,' said Jesus somewhat proudly, 'there are many rooms. I would not tell you this if it were not so. And I am going to prepare a place for you.'

But Thomas the doubter, not noted for believing everything he heard, failed to be convinced. 'Tell me something *real* about it,' he said.

Now, for the Jesus of John's gospel, reality comprised something rather different from the reality of Toad's world. The reality of Jesus knew nothing of the boat-house, and the fish-pond, and the old walled kitchen-garden; nothing of the pig-sties, and the stables, and the pigeon-house, and the hen-house; nothing of the dairy, and the wash-house, and the china-cupboards; nothing of the linen-presses, and the banqueting-hall.

'Tell me something *real* about it,' said Thomas the doubter, who was not noted for believing everything he heard.

Now for the Jesus of John's gospel the reality that really mattered was the reality of following where Jesus had gone before. 'I am going to prepare a place for you,' said Jesus. 'And after I go and prepare a place for you, I will come back and take you to myself, so that where I am you will be also.'

'Tell me something *real* about it,' said Thomas the doubter, who was not noted for believing everything he heard. Jesus answered him, 'You know the way that leads to the place where I am going.'

In growing exasperation Thomas the doubter, who was not noted for believing everything he heard, cried out again, 'Tell me something *real* about it. We do not know where you are going, so how can we know the way to get there?' Jesus answered him, 'I am the way, the truth, and the life; no one goes to the Father except by me.' Now there's reality for you. Perhaps even Thomas the doubter began to grasp the point that not even the description of the boat-house and the fish-pond, and the old walled kitchen-garden, and the pig-sties, and the stables, and the pigeon-house, and the hen-house and the dairy, and the wash-house, and the china-cupboards; and the linen-presses, and the banqueting-hall says all that there is to be said about what is real in the world.

There are some things that just have to be taken on trust. It is not always easy to grasp the detail.

PRAYER
Lord Jesus Christ,
you go to prepare a place for your people.
Give us grace to follow in your way,
to base our lives on your truth,
and to share in your risen life,
now and for all eternity.

Amen.

# Episode 39:
# Accepting release

*Jesus said, 'Come to me, all of you who are tired of carrying heavy loads, and I will give you rest.'*

## TOAD'S ADVENTURES

'Do be quiet a minute, Toad,' said the girl. 'You talk too much, that's your chief fault, and I'm trying to think, and you hurt my head. As I said, I have an aunt who is a washerwoman; she does the washing for all the prisoners in this castle …. . She takes out the washing on Monday morning, and brings it in on Friday evening. This is a Thursday… . I think if she were properly approached – squared, I believe, is the word you animals use – you could come to some arrangement by which she would let you have her dress and bonnet and so on, and you could escape from the castle as the official washerwoman. You're very alike in many respects – particularly about the figure.'

'We're *not*,' said the Toad in a huff. 'I have a very elegant figure – for what I am.'

'So has my aunt,' replied the girl, 'for what *she* is. But have it your own way. You horrid, proud, ungrateful animal, when I'm sorry for you, and trying to help you!'

'Yes, yes, that's all right; thank you very much indeed,' said the Toad hurriedly. 'But look here! you wouldn't surely have Mr Toad, of Toad Hall, going about the country disguised as a washerwoman!'

'Then you can stop here as a Toad,' replied the girl with much spirit. 'I suppose you want to go off in a coach-and-four!'

Honest Toad was always ready to admit himself in the wrong. 'You are a good, kind, clever girl,' he said, 'and I am indeed a proud and a stupid toad. Introduce me to your worthy aunt, if you will be so kind.'

## MATTHEW 11:28 – 30

Jesus said, 'Come to me, all of you who are tired from carrying heavy loads, and I will give you rest. Take my yoke and put it on you, and learn from me, because I am gentle and humble in spirit; and you will find rest. For the yoke I will give you is easy, and the load I will put on you is light.'

## MEDITATION

As much as he craved release from the prison cell, Toad did not find the way to freedom at all easy to grasp. You see, sometimes it is the easiest solutions that are hardest to accept.

The solution clearly lay with the gaoler's daughter, if only the Toad would pause and listen. 'Do be quiet for a minute, Toad,' said the girl. 'You talk too much, that's your chief fault.' The lesson to listen rather than to speak is no simple lesson to learn. You see, sometimes it is the easiest solutions that are hardest to accept.

The solution clearly lay with the gaoler's daughter, if only the Toad would recognise her wisdom and insight. 'You horrid, proud, ungrateful animal, when I'm sorry for you and trying to help you,' said the gaoler's daughter.

The lesson to see wisdom and insight in the lowly and powerless is no simple lesson to learn. You see, sometimes it is the easiest solutions that are the hardest to accept.

The solution clearly lay with the old washerwoman, if only the Toad would overcome his pride. 'But look here!' said the Toad. 'You wouldn't surely have Mr Toad, of Toad Hall, going about the country disguised as a washerwoman!' The lesson to replace pride with humility is no simple lesson to learn. You see, sometimes it is the easiest solutions that are the hardest to accept.

The solution clearly lay with the old washerwoman, if only the Toad would see true elegance in all its rich diversity. 'You're very alike in many respects,' said the girl, 'particularly about the figure.' 'We're *not*,' said the Toad in a huff. 'I have a very elegant figure – for what I am.' The lesson to see others as we wish others to see us is no simple lesson to learn. You see, sometimes it is the easiest solutions that are the hardest to accept.

The solution clearly lay with accepting an offer freely made, if only the Toad would recognise his true need. 'Then you can stop here as a Toad,' replied the girl with much spirit. The lesson to accept a gift so freely given is no simple lesson to learn. You see, sometimes it is the easiest solutions that are the hardest to accept.

As much as he craved release from the prison cell, Toad did not find the way to freedom at all easy to grasp. Toad saw that the preacher was speaking, but failed to listen to the words. 'Do be quiet for a minute, Toad,' said the preacher. 'You talk too much, that's your chief fault.' But, thus challenged, Toad paused to hear.

As much as he craved release from the prison cell, Toad did not find the way to freedom at all easy to grasp. Toad heard the invitation from the preacher who was gentle and humble in spirit, but failed to embrace humility himself. 'You horrid, proud, ungrateful animal,' said the preacher. 'You're far too proud, that's your chief fault.' But, thus challenged, Toad lay aside his pride.

As much as he craved release from the prison cell, Toad did not find the way to freedom at all easy to grasp. Toad heard the invitation from the preacher, saying 'Take my yoke and put it on you,' but failed to welcome the prospect. 'You wouldn't surely have Mr Toad, of Toad Hall, going about the country wearing a yoke!' said he. But, thus challenged, Toad placed the yoke around his neck.

You see, sometimes it is the easiest solutions that lead to freedom. Pray that you, too, will accept that easy yoke and, accepting it, find yourself released from the prison walls that hem you in on every side.

PRAYER
Lord Jesus Christ,
your yoke is easy
and your burden is light.
Place your yoke upon us now
so that we who are weary
may find refreshment in you,
for you are our God,
now and always.

Amen.

# Episode 40:
# Experiencing freedom

*Jesus said, 'Go back and tell John what you are hearing and seeing.'*

TOAD'S ADVENTURES

With a quaking heart, but as firm a footstep as he could command, Toad set forth cautiously on what seemed to be a most hare-brained and hazardous undertaking; but he was soon agreeably surprised to find how easy everything was made for him ... . The washerwoman's squat figure in its familiar cotton print seemed a passport for every barred door and grim gateway; even when he hesitated, uncertain as to the right turning to take, he found himself helped out of his difficulty by the warder at the next gate, anxious to be off to his tea, summoning him to come along sharp and not keep him waiting there all night. The chaff and the humorous sallies to which he was subjected, and to which, of course, he had to provide prompt and effective reply, formed, indeed, his chief danger; for Toad was an animal with a strong sense of his own dignity ... . However, he kept his temper, though with great difficulty, suited his retorts to his company and his supposed character, and did his best not to overstep the limits of good taste.

It seemed hours before he crossed the last court-yard,

rejected the pressing invitations from the last guardroom, and dodged the outspread arms of the last warder, pleading with simulated passion for just one farewell embrace. But at last he heard the wicket-gate in the great outer door click behind him, felt the fresh air of the outer world upon his anxious brow, and knew that he was free!

MATTHEW 11:2 – 6

When John the Baptist heard in prison about the things that Christ was doing, he sent some of his disciples to him. 'Tell us,' they asked Jesus, 'are you the one John said was going to come, or should we expect someone else?'

Jesus answered, 'Go back and tell John what you are hearing and seeing: the blind can see, the lame can walk, those who suffer from dreaded skin-diseases are made clean, the deaf hear, the dead are brought back to life, and the Good News is preached to the poor. How happy are those who have no doubts about me!'

MEDITATION

Surely the good news that the prisoner longs to hear is nothing less than the promise of freedom, the proclamation of release.

The Toad had languished immured in the dank and noisome prison cell. Shut away by himself, he experienced all the uncertainty of self-doubt, all the despair of inescapable doom. Separated from the life for which he longed, he could do nothing other than dream of his hearth and home. Surely the good news that the prisoner longs to hear is nothing less than the promise of freedom, the proclamation of release.

Languishing immured in the dank and noisome prison cell, the Toad at long last commissioned the gaoler's daughter to seek news of the outer world. And news came back concerning the washerwoman's plan. This washerwoman's gospel carried the firm promise of freedom, the clear proclamation of release.

Languishing immured in the dank and noisome prison cell, the Toad put on the fresh garments of salvation and stepped out, with a quaking heart, but as firm a footstep as he could command. Putting on the fresh garments of salvation, the Toad stepped out to freedom. Feeling the fresh air of the outer world upon his anxious brow, the Toad knew that he was free.

Surely the good news that the prisoner longs to hear is nothing less than the promise of freedom, the proclamation of release.

John the Baptist had languished immured in Herod's dank and noisome prison cell. Shut away by himself, surely even John the Baptist experienced all the uncertainty of self-doubt, all the despair of inescapable doom. Separated from the mission field for which he longed, surely even John the Baptist could do nothing other than dream of his Lord and Saviour. Surely the good news that the prisoner longs to hear is nothing less than the promise of freedom, the proclamation of release.

Languishing immured in Herod's dank and noisome prison cell, even John the Baptist at long last commissioned his disciples to seek news of the outer world. And news came back concerning Jesus' plan. This saviour's gospel carried the firm promise of freedom, the clear proclamation of release. But it brought no set of clothes from the washerwoman's basket, no immediate key to the prison cell.

Languishing immured in Herod's dank and noisome prison cell, surely John the Baptist longed to hear the good news of Isaiah, chapter 61. 'He sent me to bring good news to the oppressed, to bind up the broken-hearted, to proclaim liberty to the captives, and release to the prisoners.' But, instead, the message of Jesus was cut short.

Go back and tell John what you are hearing and seeing: the blind can see and the lame can walk. Now here, indeed, is the proclamation of release brought by the Kingdom of God.

Go back and tell John what you are hearing and seeing: those who suffer from dreaded skin diseases are made clean and the dead are brought back to life. Now here, indeed, is the proclamation of release brought by the Kingdom of God.

Go back and tell John what you are hearing and seeing: the good news is preached to the poor. Now here, indeed, is the proclamation of release brought by the Kingdom of God.

Surely the good news that John the Baptist longs to hear is nothing less than the promise of God's reign, the proclamation of the Kingdom. You, too, can hear that proclamation and live that new freedom.

PRAYER
Lord Jesus Christ,
you bring the good news of God's Kingdom.
Set us free from the prison cells of unbelief
and give us grace to enjoy
the freedom of the people of God,
now and always.

Amen.